ABORTION: THE MASS MURDER OF CHILDREN

FIRST PRINTING

Billy Crone

Cover Design:
Chris Taylor

To my sister, Heather.

If ever there was two people,
who knew firsthand
the ravages of spiritual warfare,
It would be you and me.

Prior to salvation,
both of us,
at various times,
have danced with the devils,
played their games,
and sang their songs.

We ingested their poison,
believed their lies,
and even tried to end these lives,
multiple times.

But God did what only He can do.
He rescued us from the dominion of darkness,
He saved us from the clutches of the evil one.
He set us free.

Thank you for not only putting up with me,
and for being a wonderful sister here on earth,
but for now being a fellow soldier of Christ,
fighting the good fight,
in this greatest battle of all,
The Satanic War on the Christian.

Don't ever give up Heather,
We know who wins.

I love you.

Contents

Preface

In light of recent events and frankly, infanticide, that our country is openly endorsing, I thought now would be a good time to begin a study on abortion, the mass murdering of children. This study is video driven. I will interject some things and basically start from scratch. We are going to discuss a clip from a video called "The Voice of John." The reason this lady worked to put this video together was because she was a nurse and she came across a baby that survived an abortion attempt and she named him John. He died in her hands. But before he died, she told him that one day his story would be heard. That is the premise of what you are going to see here. This chapter is going to be on just twenty minutes of the video, because basically I want to back it all up and see how we as a people, certainly as a nation, could ever endorse something like the mass murder of children, and believe it or not, it's how we believe. What we believe determines how we behave. A lot of it is out of the lie of evolution, as you are going to see. We did a 42 week on it here at Sunrise, three years ago. Evolution produces things like this. It produces abortion. You don't really believe it is a child, it is just a blob of tissue. We are going to see how that was the rise of what Hitler did with the Jewish people. We will also look at the Eugenics movement. That was what gave birth to Planned Parenthood and Margaret Sanger who was not only a racist, but she developed Planned Parenthood to get rid of the lesser races. We will deal with that as well. Chapter One will be more of a foundation of that and the next chapter will be on the millions and millions of dollars these people are making off the mass murder of children. It's frankly sick. To a lot of you, it's going to be troubling to read, but it's something that we need to get equipped on. And I think that as long as we put our heads in the sand on this issue, we aren't doing anyone, including these children, a favor. So that's where we begin, more of a historic perspective. We are going to get into a little more of the evolution lie, as to why and how these people want to justify that it is not an actual child. Make sense? Okay, let's get started. But before we do, one last piece of advice. When you are through reading this book then will you please READ YOUR BIBLE? I mean that in the nicest possible way. Enjoy, and I'm looking forward to seeing you someday!

Billy Crone
Las Vegas, Nevada
2019

Chapter One

The History of Abortion

Why is the wrath of God being revealed from Heaven? As we are basically going to see, it's because we are making the same mistake as the Roman culture did back then. That even though you know God exists, you come up with a lie and you begin to worship created things instead of the creator, which, by the way, is the basis of evolution. You suppress the truth about God's existence, which is once again what the lie of evolution does, and then once you do that and people buy into it, then it starts going downhill until we get to that final stage, which I believe is where we are at now as a country, at that final stage where you do things that you ought not to do. And murdering one and one-half billion children, is something you ought not to do, amongst other things. So, let's take a look at why the wrath of God is being revealed.

Romans 1:18-32: "The wrath of God is being revealed from heaven against all the godlessness and wickedness of men who suppress the truth by their wickedness, since what may be known about God is plain to them. For since the creation of the world, God's invisible qualities, his eternal power and divine nature, have been clearly seen, being understood from what has been made, so that men are without excuse."

You're not going to get up there and say I didn't have enough proof. Look at creation, we dealt with this for 10 weeks in our Intelligent Design study. You see, to design something implies what? It implies a designer. If I say I found a watch in the ditch and I'm convinced that it evolved over the natural processes of wind, rain, and erosion, over millions of years, that a lightning bolt struck this rock and out popped this watch, what would you say? Time to get a new preacher. Of course, that's because watches don't design themselves. A watch has about twelve moving parts, our bodies have fifty to one hundred trillion cells. All of our organs have to be fully functional, all at the same time or you are dead meat. That's common-sense, I don't even have to open a science book. You are without a rag of excuse.

Then Paul even goes further in Romans Chapter 2. You have the light of conscience. Why do you have this knowledge of right and wrong? Even the gentiles, anyone that is not a Jew, which would be us, they don't have a Bible, but they know it is wrong to murder, where did that come from? It came from a universal law giver, God. That's why there are universal laws. You know it is wrong to murder, including children, and we will eventually see every lady that goes through that, they know immediately that it is wrong.

"For although they knew God, they neither glorified him as God nor gave thanks to him, but their thinking became futile and their foolish hearts were darkened. Although they claimed to be wise…", Now isn't that the evolutionary establishment? You dumb, dumb, we smart, smart, we have a degree, right? I don't care how many degrees you have, you and I both know there is a God, you are just trying to intellectually explain it away, but you still have no excuse.

"…they became fools and exchanged the glory of the immortal God for images made to look like mortal man and birds and animals and reptiles." Isn't that what evolution says, we came from the goo to the zoo to me and you? That's where we all came from? Instead of God, created in the image of God, you say we didn't come from Adam, we came from an ape. It's the same thing. We are going in the same pattern.

"Therefore, God gave them over in the sinful desires of their hearts to sexual impurity for the degrading of their bodies with one another. They exchanged the truth of God for a lie and worshiped and served created things rather than the Creator, who is forever praised. Amen. Because of this, God gave them over to shameful lusts." So, if you buy into the lie of evolution long enough, eventually it's going to get dark. God's going to give you over, is that what you want? Have fun, watch your society go down the tubes and it's not only going to get wicked with all kinds of immorality, but what specific form of immorality will come down the pipe next? Watch what he says:

"Even their women exchanged natural relations for unnatural ones. In the same way the men also abandoned natural relations with women and were inflamed with lust for one another. Men committed indecent acts with other men and received in themselves the due penalty for their perversion." What's he talking about? Homosexuality and Lesbianism. So here he says, once you buy into the lie, dare I say evolution, that becomes the mindset of the people, you're not only going to start doing immoral things but eventually your society is actually going to be open to celebrating and promoting homosexuality which is what we see today.

Evolution was introduced into our secular school system in the 1960's and then it really started taking over the textbooks. Right? You still had some prayer, Bible reading, and the Ten Commandments in schools but that was all taken away gradually. What happened in the 1960's? Was that a great moral time in the history of our country? No, that was stage one. Do you think that was by chance? No, we went immediately into that sexual immoral culture, right? You call it, hippy, free love, flower power, whatever you want. That is when that all began. Now, what began to take place just two decades later? In the 1980's and 90's? Homosexuality. It's like someone is following a script. An unfortunate script, because they won't listen to God. Now he says, if you keep that up...

"Furthermore, since they did not think it worthwhile to retain the knowledge of God, he gave them over to a depraved mind, to do what ought not to be done. They have become filled with every kind of wickedness, evil, greed, and depravity. They are full of envy, murder, strife, deceit and malice. They are gossips, slanderers, God-haters, insolent, arrogant and boastful; they invent ways of doing evil; they disobey their parents; they are senseless, faithless, heartless, ruthless. Although they know God's righteous decree that those who do such things deserve death, they not only continue to do these very things but also approve of those who practice them."

And that is what we see going on right now. Not only do we live in a country that is supposed to be a Christian nation, that approves homosexuality, but now we are in a country that laws are on the books to try to protect the life of children not only in the womb, but now what's happening is it is even outside the womb, you don't even have any protection for that. That ought not to be done. But our society is approving that. That's the final stage. We're in that final stage.

So that's the Biblical basis. You wonder why the wrath of God is coming? We are following a bad script, number one. Now let's go to a video transcript of a movie called *The Voice of John*. This is the basis for the mindset, the evolutionary mindset, what it produces, and why people use that lie to do what ought not to be done.

Maryann Lawhon "*It wasn't until 1977 when I was living in West Virginia and I was working at a University teaching hospital. I had initially done one year in college and while it was a wonderful experience, people died every day. So, after a year I decided it was time to make a change and I would do obstetrical nursing where I would see life in the beginning, new life coming into the world. It was on my orientation, my first days at the teaching hospital, and I was given a little clipboard saying to make sure you do this, this, and this.*

So, I was following the clipboard. I would go in and make sure everything was set up for surgery, go into another room to make sure everything was set up for a delivery. Then I went into what is called the 'dirty utility room' to make sure it had been cleaned up from the shift before and I heard a sound that is imprinted into my heart. It was just like a little purring sound and I turned the light on and there on this dirty utility counter was a child. I ran out to get help. There were doctors and nurses sitting at the nurse's station having coffee.

I told them that I found a baby laying on the dirty utility counter. And the doctor said it was an abortion, just let it go, it's an abortion. At that time, I could only think it must have been a miscarriage and I thought that maybe I just imagined that it moved and that I heard something. I went back and looked. When I realized that no one would help me, I picked up the baby and I said I baptize you John, in the name of the Father, the Son, and the Holy Spirit and I gave that child back to the Lord. Before he died, I had the opportunity to hold him and I told him I would like everybody to know what he went through and what I saw that day in the dirty utility room."

The voice of Margaret Sanger: "*I think the greatest sin in the world is bringing children into the world when they are diseased from their parents, they have no chance in the world to be a human being.*"

Newscaster: "*Good Evening, the Supreme Court ruling today legalized abortions. With the majority of cases from Texas and Georgia settled the decision.*"

One Woman's Opinion: *"It's just a glob of cells that cannot exist outside the woman's body."*

Obama: *"If they make a mistake, I don't want them punished with a baby."*

A woman on the street: *"It's the decision of the woman, depending on the circumstances in her life, to choose to have the child or not."*

A man on the street: *"One person decides that life begins at conception, that's their opinion. But I, as a different human being, can decide otherwise."*

Reporter: *"Since January 22, 1973 over 55 million so-called fetuses have been aborted by their mother for various reasons, from inconvenience to the possible death of the mother from complications during pregnancy. Since then there has been an ongoing debate as to whether abortion is murder or an unfortunate necessity in our society. As our world presses towards the future it will only be told what that future is by the choices that we, as a society, make. So, the question remains. When does life begin?"*

Cathy Rapp, PA Searle Representative: *You know, when I was a young girl, in my early twenties, when Roe vs Wade was passed, prior to that time in our society, with the young women, you never heard the term 'a blob of tissue' or heard 'fetus.' When a young girl or mother was pregnant, she was having a baby."*

Ken Ham, President and Founder of Answers in Genesis, U.S.: *"At the point of conception when the sperm fertilizes the egg. You have a fertilized egg. All the information for that unique human being is right there. It's a unique combination of information. It's a different combination of information from the mother and the father to make it a unique individual. From the perspective of science, we know that at the point of conception we have a human being.*

Dr. Georgia Perdom: *"Life begins at conception so when the egg and sperm unite and become one, that is the beginning of an individual life that then grows in the womb. The only difference between you and me when I was a baby in the womb is one is bigger than the other. We have a different stage of development. There essentially is no difference because it is life and we know that from the scripture we were both fearfully and wonderfully made. In the book of Jeremiah*

God talks about how He ordained Jeremiah as a prophet before he was born. He knew He had a purpose and plan for his life.

Jeremiah 1:5: "Before I formed you in the womb, I knew you, before you were born, I set you apart; I appointed you as a prophet to the nations."

In the scripture Isaiah talks about how God has created everybody for His Glory.

Isaiah 43:7*:* "everyone who is called by my name, whom I created for my glory, whom I formed and made."

So, we know that He, especially when we read Psalm 139, that He is purposing and planning for that individual life that is going to be created by that mom and dad. So, it used to be that when you read in medical dictionaries, when they say conception, it is the beginning of life, and now it's changed."

Bodie Hodge: "*Now they say, let's go in and they actually switched the definition of conception. This is a great way to fool everybody. Most people don't realize the standard for medicine in this medical dictionary. In the 26th edition you can read what it says under conception. It's the time when the egg and sperm combine, it's basic fertilization. But guess what, the 27th edition of the medical dictionary they redefined the meaning of conception. What they said was, it is no longer the act of conceiving or fertilization. According to the 27th edition, let me read it to you, 'the act of conceiving the implantation of the blastocyst and the endometrium.' They say it is no longer the sperm and egg combining. They say it's the sperm and egg combining, and then it has to move down to implant in the uterus."*

Dr. Georgia Perdom: "*Activists are trying and asking when does life begin because they want to say at this point, they want to murder a child. In fact, some individuals say it happens after birth. We're not even talking abortion here, we are talking actual murder outside the womb, so to speak, of individuals because they feel it's ok, sometimes even up to 2 or 3 years old, it's ok to do away with them if there's something wrong, it's just not convenient any more or for whatever reason, that should be allowable."*

Cathy Rapp: *"It is very perplexing to me that in the law of man it is fine to abort a child on this day then illegal the next. Which is why we have people in the medical profession over in England debating whether or not we should have* *abortion after birth. I was interviewed by BBC right after two people from Oxford decided that if we allow abortion in the womb, why not allow abortion after birth? Why not allow sex selection? Why not allow after birth abortion? To me, there is a fine line there and we are on that slippery slope."*

Dr. Francis Schell, MD: *"With a partial birth abortion, the abortionist finds the position of the baby inside the womb using ultrasound, and he reaches inside the womb with a set of forceps, essentially a large set of pliers, so he can grasp the feet of the baby. He then drags the baby out of the womb, out of the birth canal feet first, so in the end only the head is left inside the mother. With the head still inside the mother the abortionist would stick scissors into the baby's neck right at the cranium, at the back of his skull, and make a hole. When this is done, the baby will do what anyone would do when startled with pain, he will extend his legs, he will extend his feet and hands, then the abortionist would put a suction tip in the hole and drive it into the brain and suck out the brain. The baby goes limp and the baby is removed.*

Maryann Lawhon: *I think it's evident that when we talk about partial birth abortion, the pro abortionist has no regard for the child. They have one mind set. And what really is evident is that partial birth abortion as C. Everett Coop, our former Surgeon General, said "is never necessary for the life of the mother." Technology today has given us the ability to treat the fetus in utero. And not only that, when it is necessary to abort, we can recreate the womb through medical advancements. We have incubation, we have high technology for meeting the needs so the child can continue to grow and develop outside the womb.*

Dr. Georgia Perdom *"I think there has been a big lie that has been promulgated through Planned Parenthood and those pro-choice people in our society that have tried to ease the conscience of women by saying that it's just a blob of tissue, it's a fetus, just have the procedure, go home, and go on with your life.*

Dr. Georgia Perdom: *"Charles Darwin was a naturalist in the mid to late 1800's and he is really the father of evolution by natural selection in the sense that he really promoted and popularized that idea. He gave the mechanism for the idea of evolution that all living things have basically evolved from a simple organism over a period of millions and billions of years to be all the living things that we have today. That was basically what he championed. He sought to remove God from the equation. His one daughter, Annie, died at a very young age and it had a great impact on him in the sense of 'how can a living God' and* *he would see nature, and he just couldn't see how there could be a good God in all of that. So, one of the things he sought to do was to try to eliminate Him."*

Bodie Hodge: *"One of the things that Darwin stated in his book 'The Descent of Man' in 1871, was that the Caucasians were simply superior, and they should exterminate all other races. Now think of that from an evolutionary perspective. What they are thinking is that you keep evolving and evolving and then you get the Caucasians up here on top and you should exterminate the others so there's no competition for them. And you know what? He actually made the statement that not even centuries would pass before people would start to exterminate these others."*

Dr. Alveda King: *"The founder of Planned Parenthood, initially the birth control league that became Planned Parenthood, Margaret Sanger, was a colleague and associate of people who were closely connected to Adolph Hitler. And as Hitler was learning and becoming the most diabolical processor of genocide and eugenics through what happened in the horrible holocaust of the Jews, millions of Jews that were slaughtered, Margaret Sanger was studying it."*

Dr. Georgia Perdom: *"Margaret Sanger was a social activist, a women's rights activist who was the founder of Planned Parenthood. She was born in 1879 and became active in this area in the 1900's and she founded the American Birth Control League in 1921 and then it became Planned Parenthood in the 1940's. She was a member of the socialist party. She was very much attracted to the party's fight for women's liberation of sexual desires and birth control and just really liberating, so to speak, women completely. She was very much a eugenicist too. Eugenics is a term not a lot of people are familiar with. It basically means 'well born' or born with certain desirable characteristics that society considers desirable. For example, to the Nazis and Hitler it was blond hair and blue eyes. For many societies it means not having certain diseases or deformities. So she was a eugenicist and with Planned Parenthood, that was what she started to promote, those eugenic ideas because she felt that helping the poor and helping the sick, helping the diseased was really degrading the human race and that humans could very much evolve to a higher plane or higher level if they could just get rid of the undesirable, so to speak."*

Dr. Alveda King: "*And so Dr. Sanger in the United States of America began to use some of those practices. She stood and spoke to a group or gathering of the Ku Klux Klan and educated them on how to conduct some types of genocide and* *eugenics and that it was very important to practice population control. The population that Dr. Sanger, in America, in the 1920's or so, she wanted to control the Negro population. She said colored people are like weeds and they need to be exterminated."*

Dr. Georgia Perdom: *"Margaret Sanger, and there was no doubt she felt that the other races that were not Caucasian were genetically inferior and she says that. A lot of people tend to make her out not to be a racist, but her writings are freely available online and you can read them, and you can see from that, that she felt every race that was not Caucasian was genetically inferior. She wanted to basically decrease those populations over time and so that is why she opened up a lot of these birth control clinics in areas that were mainly populated by people of other nationalities.*

There is no doubt that she believed in evolution. There were quotes from her that she again wanted man to progress to a higher evolution if these types of things that she was suggesting were implemented. In her journal, 'The Birth Control Review' one of the tag lines was at one point, 'Birth control to create a race of thoroughbreds.' Her eugenic goals were very, very, clear in that.

Eugenics, the foundation of it, is evolution, it comes from that, the practical application of that, essentially to man, saying that if evolution is true, this is what we need to do to make sure man continues to evolve. So, Hitler took it to an extreme level in a sense that he didn't just want to just control the birth of certain people, he was just going to murder them to get rid of them completely. So, it's sort of that extreme side of eugenics which is just a natural outpouring of that."

Bodie Hodge: *"What Adolph Hitler was thinking, and the Nazis, they were thinking along the same line, Caucasians on top, but they took it one step further. They took the Aryans out of the Caucasians that were on top. So, everybody else should be exterminated. They had targets for Jews, they had targets for the Poles and a number of others, of course the Jews took the brunt of it.*

If you look at it, he was thinking from an evolutionary world view, that they were a superior race, and that they needed to exterminate everyone else. A direct reflection of what Darwin taught in his book "The Descent of Man." Now think of that repercussion ever since. Look at World War Two, look at the number of deaths as a direct result of that. Other famous evolutionists, Joseph Stalin, it was estimated twenty-million people died, just because of Joseph Stalin. Pol Pot,

Mao, look at the number of people that have died as the direct result of the evolutionary world view. We think of that in terms of war, total number of U.S. deaths from all military conflicts since the American Revolution, 834,386, people being annihilated within their countries. You know what another direct result is? The unborn. Total number of U.S. deaths from abortion since 1973, 54,559,615. When they are killed people view them as though they are just animals and that is exactly what Charles Darwin was teaching, they are just animals, why not get rid of them?"

Dr. Georgia Perdom: *"People say that eugenics just sort of died out with the Nazis and the whole idea of getting rid of a certain people group just died out. But it didn't. It just became quiet and careful. In principal, same idea's, just different means to accomplish them. And one of the ways that is happening today is obviously through abortion, through organizations like Planned Parenthood and they are still very much pursuing these eugenics ideals."*

Ken Ham: *"We live in a culture where the belief in evolution of millions of years is taught as fact in our education system and through much of the media. If you bring up generations of kids in an educational system where they have thrown God out, the Bible out, and prayer out, and you teach them that everything happens by natural process, that there is no God, that man is just an animal then that's going to greatly affect how they view issues like abortion.*

In other words, get rid of spare cats, get rid of spare kids, what's the difference? We're all animals anyway. What does it matter? If we start with the Bible, we say that God created as an absolute authority, we have the history in Genesis, that is the foundation to the rest of the Bible. The Bible is God's word, that is the foundation of the world view, then you know that abortion is killing a human being. And deliberately killing a human being like that would be wrong. And therefore, on the basis of the absolute authority we have a basis for saying that abortion is wrong."

But what was the lie that people believe? Romans Chapter 1, that started the whole process of the descent of man, it's evolution. Now, let's further explore that issue with Adolph Hitler. Adolph Hitler, one of the many horrible things he did, of course, was the Jewish holocaust. He was a mass murderer and mass murdered 6,000,000 Jews and of course these are people outside of the womb. You have to understand why he did what he did. It is the same justification they try to pull off for the mass murder of children inside the womb and dare I say what is the discussion that is going on now? Now it's even outside the womb. It's the same premise. Adolph Hitler was not only an occultist; he was an evolutionist. When you understand that, it explains why he did what he did. Again, it's what you believe that determines how you behave. Let's look at Hitler's Hit List. This is on historical record. Why did he murder the Jewish people? If he could have continued on after World War II he would have continued on with his list. It's an evolutionary hit list.

HITLER'S HIT LIST

Nordic People (blonde, blue eyed)	Close to pure Aryan
Germanic People (brown hair, blue-eyed)	Predominately Aryan
Mediterranean	Slight Aryan
Slavic People (white by degenerate bone)	Half-Aryan, half-Ape
Oriental People	Slight Ape
Black African	Predominately Ape
Jewish People (fiendish skull)	Close to pure Ape

At the top of the list he believed that the Nordic people were close to pure Aryan, with the blond hair and blue eyes. Next on the list were the Germanic people, they were brown haired, blue eyed, predominately Aryan, not as pure, but pretty close. Then there were the Mediterranean people, next on the list, they were slight Aryan according to Hitler. Slavic people, they were half Aryan, half ape. Again, how he can call somebody 'Ape?' It was the evolutionary mind set as well. Then further down the list were the Oriental people, where you can see that he considered them slight ape. Then the black Africans he considered them predominately ape. And wonder of wonders, look who is at the bottom of his 'Hit List.' It's the Jewish people. He felt that the Jewish were close to pure ape. They had a fiendish skull. So why did he start with them? Because he was starting at the bottom of the list and he would have worked his way up to who? He would have worked his way through the Oriental, Slavic, Mediterranean and German people until he had a pure Aryan race. That was his goal. Praise God, I believe God intervened and put a stop to that. But again, what's going on today? That was horrible. That was a holocaust of real people, six million. Oh, that stat we saw before of 54,000,000 babies, that was an old stat, it's over 60 million now. So, ten times the amount of people, albeit children, but they are still people, we still talk about that and rightly so. We have television programs, we have a historical record, we need to never forget that. Why aren't we dealing with something that is over ten times the amount? But it's the same premise. You buy into evolution, you buy into that lie, you start doing things that you ought not to do. In the next chapter we are going to see what it has to do with and that is money. But let's look at what Hitler believed. These are secular individuals admitting that evolution influenced Hitler into generating a Holocaust.

R. Miller: *"Encyclopedia of Evolution said: 'During the 1930's Adolf Hitler believed he was carrying Darwinism forward with his doctrine that undesirable individuals...*

And that's the problem, who gets to determine that, first of all it's wrong, we are all created in the image of God, we are all a special creation from Him, we all have a wonderful plan from God, but who gets to decide it? It's the evolutionary mind set. The strongest, the fittest, and in this case, Hitler thought, was the German people, so he thought he gets to decide, it's no different today.

"...and inferior races must be eliminated. The position in Germany was that man must 'conform' to nature's processes, no matter how ruthless. The 'fittest' must never stand in the way of the law of evolutionary progress. In its extreme form, that social view was used in Nazi Germany to justify sterilization and mass murder of the 'unfit,' 'incompetent,' 'inferior races.'"

Did you know that is going on today? Did you know they have control of children in China? It's been that way for a long time. You can't have more children than what they say you can have. Also, they are talking about sterilization. In the Obama administration, one of his health czars said that we need to start talking about forced, mass sterilization of people who cannot be responsible with children, in our own country. Oh, and by the way, Obama was actually at a meeting for Planned Parenthood and he ended it with these words, "God Bless Planned Parenthood." What was his first act on his first day in office? He opened the flood gates for abortion and for us to begin to pay for abortions, not just in our own country, but even abroad. First day in office, that tells you the mindset.

Robert Clark: *"Darwin: Before and After" said: One need not read far in Hitler's 'Mein Kompf' to find that evolution influenced him and his views on the master race, genocide, human breeding experiments, etc."*

Now why would they do stuff like that? Well they're just animals, anyway. We test products on rabbits, and monkeys, etc. for the good of mankind, well now you're talking about human beings. Well according to evolution they are just animals. They haven't evolved. They are just Jewish people, so who cares? It's the same kind of mindset. That's what it is going to produce.

Edward Simon: Another side to the Evolution Problem said: *"I cannot deny that the theory of evolution, and the atheism it engendered led to the moral climate that made a holocaust possible."*

Did you know that a law was actually put out that Jewish people were not a people? Our country is trying to put out laws that these children are not children. It's no different. Do you see the pattern? Once you buy into this lie called evolution, you wonder why we need to learn what this thing spawns. Abortion is one of the things that this spawned and it's not the only one. It's atheism, its mindset. Even though if you look at some of the photo ops Hitler did back in the day, he posed as a Christian. Do politicians do that today? Ever see those guys that, for a photo op, they just happen to be walking around with a Bible in their hands?

Adolph Hitler: *"I regard Christianity as the most fatal, seductive lie that has ever existed. He who would live must fight; he who does not wish to fight in this world where permanent struggle is the law of life, has not the right to exist."*

What does that sound like? Natural selection. Darwin. Where do you think this is all coming from? And lest you think there's any doubt that evolution empowered Hitler to do the evils that he did, then listen again to this Molecular Biologist. It's also the justification she says for evils today.

Bryan Fischer, host of Focal Point: *"It seems like you could draw a straight line from Darwin's evolution to social Darwinism, I mean if it's survival of the fittest,* *let's get rid of the weakest members of our society. It makes absolute logical sense if you believe in Darwinism, this is how all of life develops, this is how we keep getting increasingly complex life forms. So, it seems like you can draw almost a straight line between Charles Darwin and Margaret Sanger, the eugenics movement and Adolph Hitler. But you have pretty much a broken line from the theory of evolution to Hitler's Germany. Is that an over exaggeration?"*

Dr. Georgia Perdom *"No, it's not. It's absolute. And that is one of the things that I'll be showing in a presentation that I will be doing with the Life Series to show that building from Charles Darwin to Francis Dalton to Margaret Sanger to Nazi Germany and all those others in this one big continuum so to speak. One thing leads to another. When we start compromising on the Bible in one part, like the idea of evolution, it's just another step on another part, like the sanctity of life."*

So again, if you buy into evolution what does it produce? Here's a little teaser from our evolution study of 42 weeks, it's called *The Witness of Creation.* I'm going to share a little teaser of the one section called *A Special Creation: Exposing the Lie of Evolution,* and there is no evidence, it's all based on lies. One of the lies they try to use to justify abortion and eugenics, once again is to say it is not a baby, it's just a blob of tissue. Well that was started by a German evolutionist, Ernst Haeckel, in the late 1800's.

"*The idea of embryology"* (Ontogeny Recapitulates Phylogeny), as he says, "*is that a fertilized egg develops to form an embryo, it actually repeats its evolutionary history."*

So here is what he did. Haeckel actually examined and drew pictures of fish, frogs, chickens, pigs and human embryos side by side and said there was a remarkable similarity between their stages of development. Therefore, he said, "*it was these supposed similarities that provided a 'silent moving picture' of our evolutionary past.*" Because remember, we all came from the same supposedly blob of goo, to the zoo, to me and you, and that is why it is so similar with all these embryo developments. So, to help propagate his new 'religion,' Haeckel drew enormous backdrops of pictures of his embryos and toured from city to city to the point where it was called a sort of "Darwinian passion play." He would go around and tell people what he had found in all the evidence of evolution and embryology. Now believe it or not, his lie affected and was caught on by Hitler. Charles Darwin believed it was Haeckel's enthusiasm that was the main reason for Germany's acceptance of evolution.

Because again, when Darwin came out, there was still a strong Judeo-Christian ethic and it took a while for it to catch on. They were always scrambling for the so-called missing link. So, the problem with the missing link is, guess what? It's still missing and will always be missing because there is no link between man and ape. When this came out, when they are looking for this missing link, he comes up with this embryology thing and says, "Look, they are all similar and that proves evolution." Germany bought into it and then it began to go crazy.

But Haeckel didn't stop there. He even came up with a new missing link, which he called Pithecanthropus alalus or the 'speechless ape-man.' There is zero evidence. You just make a drawing and somehow it becomes true. Now, believe it or not, in many textbooks today, that's all there is. The only evidence of evolution is in people's minds and in the textbooks. He even had an artist draw the imagined creature and his supposed wife. Later a Dutch scientist concluded that since neither one of them could speak, *"It must have been a happy marriage because his wife couldn't contradict him."*

So much so was this idea of Haeckel's embryology accepted that we still see its influence today behind such things as Freudian psychology. Freud was an atheist and an evolutionist, and he was a cocaine addict. He was a promoter of cocaine and he was addicted to nicotine which led to his death. He smoked 20 to 30 cigars a day and he refused to be psychoanalyzed by Carl Jung. Carl Jung was involved in mysticism. He admitted that his ideas came from these voices that he heard which were coming from demons. He called one Philemon and one was Basilaties. This is where he got his inspiration from. He felt evil in the room. And we are supposed to listen to these guys? So now, not only did evolution influence Hitler, but it also influenced Freud. Freud believed that in order to understand dysfunctional behavior we need to understand our "earlier stages of evolutionary development."

But that's not all. We also see it in the beliefs of the popular modern child specialist Dr. Spock. Remember him? He was the big rage; he knows better than the rest of us as to how to discipline our children. This guy is an evolutionist, and we are supposed to listen to him?

Dr. Spock: "*Each child, as he develops, is retracing the whole history of mankind, physically and spiritually, step by step. A baby starts off in the womb as* *a single tiny cell just the way the first living thing appeared in the ocean. Weeks later, as he lies in the amniotic fluid of the womb, he has gills like a fish."*

I don't know if you have ever been bit by a toddler with that first tooth, it hurts, but he didn't come from a shark. That's the lie of evolution. Remember what the evolutionists say, we came from the goo from the ocean, to the zoo with the animals, to me and you. It's a bunch of baloney. If he can't even get the origin right, why would I listen to anything else that he had to say? And oh, by the way, how is secular psychology working out for folks? It's not. You look at the secular psychologists and their own personal lives. Not to mention that they push all kinds of drugs that actually produce suicide and other bad stuff. By the way, when we first started listening to, not the Biblical way to discipline our children, but we started listening to the secular way to discipline our children, how has our society turned out? Kids have gone nuts, you can't touch them because you will damage their self-esteem, blah, blah, blah.

And then just in case there's any doubt, as recent as 1986, the Reader's Digest Book of Facts stated that Haeckel's theory of embryology *really is an established fact*. Well there is a big problem with that theory. The problem with all those pictures and diagrams of embryos that Haeckel used for proof of his theory was they were ***fakes***. As it turns out, Haeckel was an accomplished artist as well as an anatomist. He faked the drawings to make his theory appear to be true! It's like in the area of natural selection, we did the study of the peppered moths, the black and white moths, and then over the years black soot from the factories came, this is all in the textbooks today, the white moths originally were dominant, but then the black ones became dominant because of all the soot. The soot from the factories colored them, but then when they shut down the factories, and the air started to get cleaned up, the black ones were evident on the trees and the birds ate them and that was supposed to be proof of natural selection. Do you know what the real thing was? Kettelwell said in all those years, he only saw two moths in existence at night, not in the day when he took pictures of them, which is what is now in the textbooks. The pictures that he did use were fake because he captured some, he put them in the refrigerator, and he had to pin them or glue them to the tree. Before that, most of them were dying but some were just barely alive and sluggish, so he had to put them on his car to warm them up. It's the same thing with this Haeckel theory. It's all fake but it's been a lie for a long time. It was exposed as a fraud a long time ago.

Believe it or not, his phony pictures and data were exposed as frauds as early as 1874. For instance, at the top of Haeckel's phony drawings is a dog and human embryo in his book *The History of Creation*. But the actual photographs are down below, and they are incredibly, radically different. That's how well he faked it. Let me give you another one. In this picture you see at the top how much he manipulated the facts, his drawings of different animals' embryos and the real ones are at the bottom, the actual embryos.

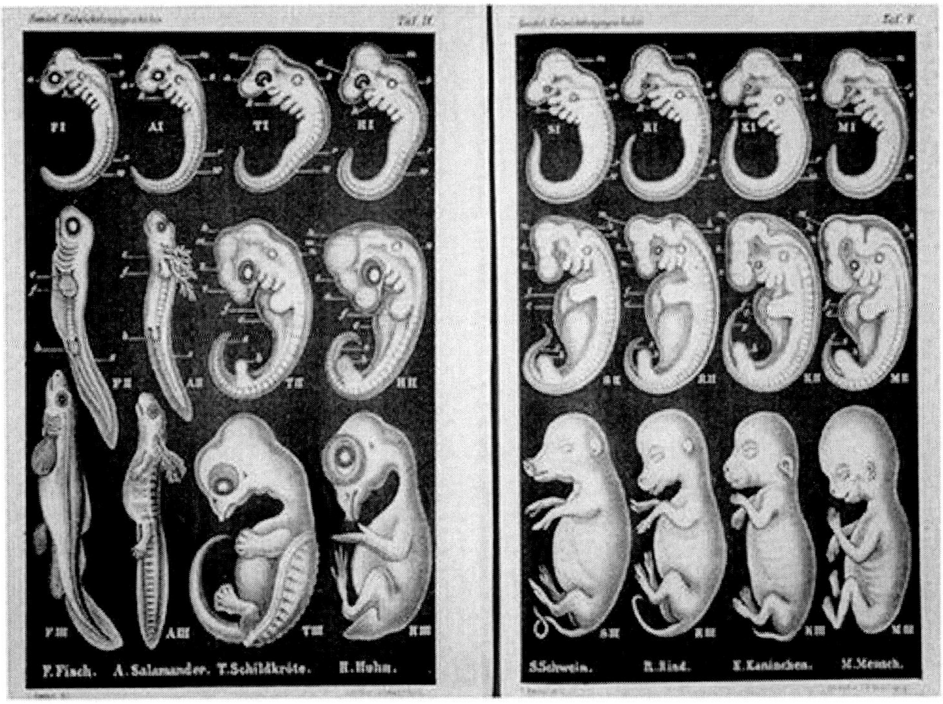

Do you see how far off he is? What a liar! It's not even close because there is no proof of evolution, it's a lie. They're not only severely different, but Haeckel obviously severely altered them to get his 'desired' results. Not only were Haeckel's drawings exposed as frauds in 1874, but he was also convicted of this fraud by his own university. At Jena, the university where he taught, he was charged with fraud by five professors and convicted by the university court and as a result, Haeckel was considered a disgrace for the remainder of his career. However even after clearly being guilty and convicted of this fraud, Haeckel still blamed others for his behavior saying, "*Other evolutionists had committed similar offenses.*" Makes you wonder what else they're lying about! Believe it or not, in spite of the fact that Haeckel's drawings were proven a complete fake back in 1874, they are still in many Biology textbooks today! Soapbox time… home school, Christian school, get your kids out of the sewer pipe, they are being lied to. Why am I bringing this up? Because this is the evolutionary lie that people use to justify the mass murder of children because according to Haeckel it's just a blob of tissue retracing its evolutionary past. It's not a real child, it's a lie. Let me give you some examples. The last picture is supporting Haeckel's theory from a textbook called *Biology Sixth Edition 2004 by Raven and Johnson*. Now either the authors are ignorant of the truth or they're deliberately lying to promote their religion of evolution. In fact, embryologist Michael Richardson said in *Science Magazine*: *"Sadly, it is the discredited 1874 drawings that are used in so many British and American biology textbooks. Therefore, believe it or not, the fraud continues!"*

The next explosive thing is that the evolutionists admit that Haeckel's drawings were a lie.

Dr. Stephen J. Gould admitted that: *"Haeckel has exaggerated the similarities between embryos of different species and his drawings never fooled expert embryologists who recognized his fudgings right from the start. Haeckel's drawings, despite their noted inaccuracies, entered into the most impenetrable and permanent of all quasi-scientific literatures: standard student textbooks of biology. We do, I think, have the right to be both astonished and ashamed by the century of mindless recycling that has led to the persistence of these drawings in a large number, if not a majority of modern textbooks!"*

Zoologist L. Rutimeyer of Basle University called Haeckel's distorted drawings *'a sin against scientific truthfulness.'*

Dr. Michael Richardson, an embryologist at St. George Medical School in London said: *"This is one of the worst cases of scientific fraud. It's shocking to find that somebody once thought of as a great scientist is deliberately misleading. It makes me angry. What Haeckel did was to take a human embryo and copy it, pretending that the salamander and the pig and all the others looked the same at the same stage of development. They don't. These are fakes."*

These are people from their own camp. You would think that they would get it right. No, because as one guy said, *"If you remove all the lies that used to support evolution in the textbooks you would have no evidence of the theory of evolution."* My theory is, get rid of your lie. Because if you are doing it on purpose you are doing it to lie to the children. Because you want them to come out with this mindset.

Sir Arthur Keith stated: *"Now that the appearance of the embryo at all stages is known, the general feeling is one of disappointment. The human embryo at no stage is anthropoid in appearance. The embryo of the mammal never resembles the worm, the fish, or the reptile. Embryology provides no support whatsoever for the evolutionary hypothesis."*

Now the problem is again, what they use to justify abortion. The mass murder of children. Eventually I want to get us equipped with how to have a reasonable debate, if you will, with those people who have a different view, pro-abortion. Just to give you a little teaser, don't even use the word abortion. Don't use their terms. Their words are designed to avoid the issue and the sting of what they are really doing. I'll give you a little teaser, if someone comes up to you, and it has happened to me before. They say, *"Do you mean to tell me you are anti-abortion?"* The anti sounds bad but there is a reasoning behind it, they are hiding behind terminology. I respond, *"Yes, I am against murdering children."* That just changed the narrative just like that. Don't use their terminology. They say, *"Do you mean to tell me that a fetus has rights?"* I reply, *"Yes, I believe all children have rights."* The term fetus makes it sound like a blob of tissue and we'll get into all that later. But this is what is being used to justify it.

Here are some stats. It's a modern-day holocaust. We get in an uproar, and rightly so, about six million Jews being killed in the holocaust, but where is the conversation about this modern-day holocaust?

1. 48% of all pregnancies among American women are unintended and ½ of these potential children are killed by abortion.

2. Each year, 2 out of every 100 women, ages 15-44 have an abortion and 47% of them have already had at least 1 prior abortion.

3. An estimated 43% of women will have had at least 1 abortion by the time they are 45 years old.

4. During the Revolutionary War 25,000 Americans died. During the Civil War nearly 500,000 people died. During WWI over 100,000 people died. During

WWII over 400,000 people died. And in both the Korean and Vietnam wars about 113,000 died. However, since 1973 in the war on the unborn we have had over 60,000,000 babies murdered by abortion in America alone, and just since 1980 we have had over 1,526,000,000 babies murdered by abortion worldwide.

And what was our opening text? The wrath of God will be poured out. Do you ever wonder why the wrath of God is going to be not 7 days, 7 weeks, 7 months, but 7 years nonstop? And I think it has something to do with this. It's all based on a lie called evolution and embryology and it's now produced one of the most vicious murderous societies we've ever seen, as this recent decision shows, this is the attempt to protect children outside the womb.

These are the senators, and the bulk of them are from the Democratic party, and what did they say? They said, *"No! We will not protect a child that has been born outside the womb."* That they deserve protection, they said, *"No!"* That's why we are dealing with this now because it has gone outside the womb and it all stems from the same lie, the same mistake, Romans Chapter 1, and we better wake up because the wrath of God is coming. In the next chapter we are going to deal with the aspect of money. They have turned this into a mass killing machine to get rich. It's very sick and it's very disturbing but again, we have to deal with it.

Chapter Two

The Motive of Abortion

In the last chapter we dealt with the history of abortion, the mass murder of children. I almost don't want to use the term abortion because as I said, you don't want to use their terms. That is how they get to hide behind this stuff. It's not a fetus, it's a baby. It's not abortion, it's killing a child. That is what is really going on, right? So, we've been dealing with that aspect and we also have been looking biblically as to why and how did we get into this shape as a country, the United States of America. In Romans 1 we saw basically that once you deny the existence of God, which is what our country has done, bought into the lie, and promoted the lie, now, that is all you get in schools, you don't get options any more. It's the lie of evolution. There is no God. Then when you go down that route, what happens? You move into the next stage, and you start getting into all kinds of immorality. If you don't turn around from that, then what happens? It starts to get even worse and you start getting into homosexuality and lesbianism, the scripture is very clear about that. Then if you don't turn around from that, what happens? Man, you have moved to that final stage and you start doing things you ought not to do, and abortion is certainly one of those things you ought not to do.

We also saw that the history of it stems from not only the same trap we're falling for in Romans Chapter 1, we're going down that unfortunate spiral. We saw that historically it's based on the lie of evolution. That is not a baby it is just a blob of tissue. That's the rationale. That's how they get around this issue.

It's a lie. But we also saw what led to the belief system called Eugenics. Remember that? Eugenics is basically the mindset that we need to get rid of these lesser evolved people who are messing up the gene pool of humanity. So, we can keep ourselves clean, be the strongest and the fittest. As crazy as that is, we also saw what Hitler picked up on. That's what Hitler used to justify his Holocaust of people outside the womb called the Jewish people. It's no different, it's the same principal. You kill people inside the womb, babies, you kill people outside the womb. It's the same principal. It's the lie of evolution, there is no God, it's Eugenics, keep it clean. As we saw, historically, that is the foundation of Margaret Sanger. Margaret Sanger was a big fan of Hitler, she was also an evolutionist, and she was also a Eugenicist. That's why she started Planned Parenthood. It was to clean up the inferior races. She was a racist and she was a Eugenicist. That might sound kind of weird and kind of harsh but basically, what you are dealing with is that people who believe through the Eugenics movement, basically getting rid of the inferiors, that mankind will create his own utopia. What Hitler was involved in, the Aryan race was going to rule for a thousand years and bring all kinds of great things to the planet. Well, this is the same premise, right? But Margaret Sanger is not the only one, there's still people alive today that are big promoters of this Eugenics movement. I want to get into that before I get into the next segment. But let's start off with Margaret Sanger. It's all about getting rid of the inferiors so we can reduce the population to make a new humanity.

Margaret Sanger: *"The elimination of human weeds, for the cessation of charity because it prolonged the lives of the unfit..."*

Now remember Margaret Sanger is the founder of Planned Parenthood, the ones who are pushing abortion, the mass murder of children in our country.

Margaret Sanger: *"and for the segregation of morons, misfits, and the maladjusted, and for the sterilization of genetically inferior races."*

That's not only racist, but this is the founder of Planned Parenthood, but again she is not the only one.

David Graber, a research biologist with the National Park Service: *"We have become a plague upon ourselves and upon the earth. Human happiness is not as important as a wild and healthy planet. Until such time as us homo sapiens* *should decide to rejoin nature, some of us can only hope for the right virus to come along."*

This is crazy, but this is what people think, it's okay to get rid of mass amounts of people because we need to create our own utopia.

Jacques Cousteau: "*The damage people cause to the planet is a function of demographics, it is equal to the degree of development. One American burdens the earth much more than twenty Bangladeshis. This is a terrible thing to say. In order to stabilize world population, we must eliminate 350,000 people per day. It is a horrible thing to say, but it's just as bad not to say it."*

Now as I've said before, overpopulation is a lie. A huge lie. I joke about this. I fly all the time now and I'm in a plane a lot. So, every time I look out the window, if you think we are overpopulated at any time in your journey, look out the window. There is so much wide-open space, everywhere. Not just the United States. In Canada, in Europe, in Australia, it's wide open. There's plenty of land. Basically, it's a bunch of baloney to push this agenda. It's not overpopulated. They want you to buy into that lie by showing us pictures and saying we are overpopulated. You know what they show? The scene outside the window of the plane, that show miles and miles of open land all over the planet? No, they show downtown Beijing, in China, they show New York City, it's crazy but that's their mind set, right? Because how are you going to justify getting rid of 350,000 people per day?

Bertrand Russell: "*At present, the population of the world is increasing. War so far has had no great effect on this increase. I do not pretend that birth control is the only way in which the population can be kept from increasing. There are others. If a Black Death could be spread throughout the world once in every generation, survivors could procreate freely without making the world too full. The state of affairs might be somewhat unpleasant, but what of it? Really high-minded people are indifferent to suffering, especially that of others."*

Ted Turner: *"People who abhor the China one-child policy are dumb-dumbs, because if China hadn't had that policy, there would be 300 million more people in China right now."*

Then he later advocated that we reduce the world's population from 6 billion to 2 billion. As one guy said, okay Ted, let's start with your family. But you see it's always somebody else's family, isn't it? Because they are the rich and powerful, we are the dumb-dumbs as he said, and we don't deserve to live, only the elite.

John Holdren: Obama's Science Czar: *"Forced abortions and mass sterilizations are needed to save the planet."*

We are all hearing about this new Green Deal thing, it's crazy, but this is what people believe. It's not just getting rid of cows and their flatulence, or whatever, and it's not just about getting rid of airplanes, they want to control who lives and who dies.

John Holdren: "*Women could be forced to abort their pregnancies, whether they wanted to or not; the population at large could be sterilized by infertility drugs intentionally put into the nation's drinking water or in food. And people who contribute to social deterioration, i.e. undesirables, can be required by law to exercise reproductive responsibility, that is, be compelled to have abortions or be sterilized. A transnational Planetary Regime should assume control of the global economy and also dictate the most intimate details of Americans lives using an armed international police force."*

Dr. Eric Pianka, a scientist, gave a speech at the Texas Academy of Science where he advocated: *"The need to exterminate 90% of the population through the airborne Ebola virus. We're no better than bacteria."*

Now, why and where did he get that from? Evolution. The lie of Evolution. Again, we saw the history, where did this stuff come from? He did this standing in front of some human skulls and he gleefully advocated airborne Ebola as his preferred method of exterminating 90% of humans on the planet, choosing it over AIDS because of its faster kill period. At the end of Pianka's speech the audience erupted not to a chorus of boos and hisses but to a wild reception of applause and cheers. They gave him cheers. You see that same sickening response of people rejoicing over the death of people when the New York bill was passed for being able to kill babies all the way up until birth. And they applaud it. It's gross but it's what is going on today.

Dr. Sam Keen, a New Age writer and philosopher stated, "*We must speak far more clearly about sexuality, contraception, about abortion, about values that control the population because the ecological crisis, in short, is the population* *crisis. Cut the population by 90% and there aren't enough people left to do a great deal of ecological damage."*

Notice who is being duped into going along with this. Even the idea of population control, the idea of supporting abortion, the mass murder of children, which would also include outside the womb, which would also include adults which are getting too old. It's called euthanasia. So that the government can decide when. It's all related. They are bringing this into the environmental movement. Now what generation has been indoctrinated into this their whole life? And they are just starting to come into power. Rhymes with millennials. This is all they have ever known. It's all that's been pumped into their minds with the media, with the secular school system, and then these guys say this, we have to sacrifice our lives, other people's lives, to save the planet.

Dr. Michael Berliner wrote of the environmentalist's utter contempt for mankind *"Such is the naked essence of Environmentalism. It mourns the death of one whale or tree but actually welcomes the death of billions of people. Is there a more malevolent, manhating philosophy than this?"*

So that's what we are dealing with. I wanted to give you a little more background on this, the history, where is it coming from, why are we as a nation continuing to get worse and worse when it comes to this issue? You would think that this would have been solved a long time ago. We never should have made it through Roe vs Wade, how it ever got to the Supreme Court is beyond me. But it keeps getting worse because this stuff is continually being talked about in our school system. A whole generation is getting indoctrinated in it. You and I are looked upon as the old fuddy-duddies.

In this chapter, I not only want to deal with the history, but I want to deal with the motive. Now you notice there is sort of a religious belief, environmentalism. They treat it like a religion, they are going to save the planet. But I want to deal with the motive. Why do people persist in pushing the mass murder of children? Well, it's not only used to supposedly create an environmental utopia on the planet, but it's big, big, money and the Bible warns us about that. Better be careful. If you get all hung up on cash and that starts to rule your heart, you're probably not going to make some good decisions. And I really believe that is a big part as to why abortion, the mass murder of children, is continually pushed in our country. I Timothy 6 is on the love of money.

I Timothy 6:6-10: *But godliness with contentment...*

What is the key word here? Godliness, godliness is your walk with Jesus Christ, and you are content. God will take care of you, everything is fine, he knows what he is doing, God never says, "Oh, I can't believe you went through that, I was so surprised, I apologize from Heaven on high, I just..." No, He knows what He is doing, so have a great walk with Jesus Christ. God wants you to be content, have a great time and we haven't even got to Heaven yet, but here's the trap. The enemy is going to throw a trap at you, the enemy is going to tell you that God doesn't know what He is doing. That I'm lacking something, I need more. And he's going to say it's money. You better be careful.

...is great gain. For we brought nothing into the world, and we can take nothing out of it. But if we have food and clothing...

How many of you have eaten food today? How many have extra food at the house? How many of you have so much food at your house that you have canned items that you haven't eaten in 12 years? You have still not thrown away that can of hominy that somehow landed in your shopping cart 14 years ago. It's still there. So, we not only have food, but we have plenty of food, right? Now, how many of you are wearing clothes? I am very glad that you are. It would be a serious distraction. So, what does it say? You have food, you have clothing, life is good. So, it says we will be content with that, because this is not Heaven. Heaven comes later, right? God's taking care of us. He's good. We have what we need. We're sucking air. In fact, put your hand on somebody's mouth. Now if you feel air, guess what, they are still alive. That's good. But here is the problem. God has given us everything we need, especially here in America, come on. Be content, walk in godliness with great gain.

...we will be content with that. People who want to get rich....

Notice the content, people, content vs not enough. I need more, I need riches, I need the things of this world.

...fall into temptation and a trap and into many foolish and harmful desires that plunge men into ruin and destruction. For the love of money is the root of all kinds of evil....

Not the root of all evil, it says the root of all kinds of evil. This is so misquoted so many times, it's crazy. The love of money is the root of all kinds of evil. Who is the root of evil? Satan. But loving money will lead to all kinds of evil.

...Some people eager for money, have wandered from the faith and pierced themselves with many griefs.

Griefs or sorrows, as it says there, and boy isn't that the truth!

And that's what we are going to see. Why is this pushed so hard in our country and we know better? I think a lot of people know better. Money. The abortion industry is not only millions of dollars, it's a billion-dollar corporation. They're doing this on an assembly line and they are becoming millionaires because of it. So, let's go ahead and take a look at the next segment of the video clip of *The Voice of John,* then we'll explore deeper into just what they are doing with these children.

Carol Everett, Former Director of Afterlife Clinic: *"I believe my journey is like that of so many women. It was born out of pain and scars from abortion.*

"There is no earthly way you can deal with killing your own child. But I had that abortion 2 weeks after Roe vs Wade. I instantly knew, instantly knew that I had killed my baby. If I ventured to tell anyone that I had been bad enough to kill my child, they quickly told me that it was a woman's right to choose and it was okay. So, I think what we do with those remarks is to cause the woman to stuff her feelings. There must be something wrong with her if she feels uncomfortable with the abortion decision.

"Nothing worked in my life. I am one of those statistics that was divorced. There's a higher statistic of couples that have had abortions that are divorced than lose a child by accidental or natural means. Actually, about 75% of relationships that conceive break up within 90 days of the abortion, as my marriage did. Nothing worked anymore, but I found something that did matter. Every time I sold another woman an abortion, in some sick twisted way, if she was okay then just maybe I was okay.

"I evolved into the abortion industry. I worked for a man that owned four abortion clinics. I ran two of them and more than doubled his business. He would not share that money with me, so I took his best abortionist and recruited him,

after all, and I opened my own abortion clinic at 1645 Mockingbird Lane, Dallas, Texas. The first month we did 45 abortions, the last month we did 535 abortions. And you wonder why I remember those numbers. I didn't have a salary. I worked on straight commission, $25.00 for each abortion. So, that last month was $13,625.00, but that was not enough. I wanted to be a millionaire. And I knew how to be a millionaire. 40,000 abortions a year would make me a millionaire.

"So, I had to start selling abortions to hit that goal of 40,000 a year. How do you sell an abortion? Well, it's actually too simple. Our goal was 3 to 5 abortions between the ages 13 and 18 from every girl, so we had to get into the schools. We had to break down the natural modesty and we had to separate them from their parents and their values. The easiest way to do that is sex education.

"Now I know some people say we need to teach them how to have safe sex or safer sex but when you hear somebody say that, just say baloney. We don't take our children out and get them good and drunk and then teach them how to drive safely drunk. We give them a moral absolute, don't drink and drive. Why in the world would we compromise them in this important area of sexual morality by giving them this low moral standard to live down to rather than the most, highest and best which is abstinence until marriage which works every time? But I didn't say that.

"In Kindergarten you just put the children in a circle, and you go around the room and you ask them all a simple question, 'What do your parents say to call your private parts?' Well, you know, and I know, every family in the world has a different name for their private parts and by the time you reach the third or fourth child it is clear to those children that their parents do not know what they have.

"But we did. To the boys, 'this is what you have' and to the girls, 'this is what you have', 'don't be ashamed of your private parts.' Then you could look out on the playground and see them sharing. We have broken down their natural modesty. They are questioning what their parents really knew and we were becoming the experts. First, second and third grade agenda is slightly different, it's intercourse.

These kids are not interested in intercourse, but we used, at this time, little square books with 6 and 7-year-old nude models with diagrams showing them how to have intercourse. One book per classroom, you did not want the parents to get their hands on that book. And then in the fourth grade the children are encouraged to masturbate alone and then in groups of 4 or 5 of the same sex, I haven't figured out how that all fits in but there it is. And then in the fifth and sixth grade someone like me steps in. Now the goal is to get them sexually active and on a low dose birth control that will not work and pass out defective or second condoms that will not work.

"Now just think about that for a minute. You are passing out free condoms. Do you think they are going to buy the most expensive or the best condoms? No, they buy defective, they buy seconds and they pass those out and when the girls come in to our clinic we gave them low dose birth control pills that we knew, that in order to provide any level of protection, they had to be taken accurately, the same time every single day. If there is one thing we know about teenagers, and you know it too, they don't do anything at the same time every day.

"You give her this birth control pill, tell her to take it every day at the same time, her mother doesn't tell her to take it, no one tells her to take it, she takes it sporadically, if she even takes it every day. Sexual activity increases from zero, once a week, to 4 or 5 time a week, the pill will not work, and we would accomplish our goal of 3 to 5 abortions between the ages of 13 and 18.

"So now she's pregnant. She's going to call our clinic because she has that card. Free pregnancy tests, licensed counselors, we were the experts. We were the ones that helped her get on the birth control pills, we could help her with her choices now. The problem is, we didn't have choices, we only had one product and we sold it well, abortion and abortion only.

"When she called our clinic, we had a phone script, actually a script used by telemarketers. We called them telephone counselors, but they were trained as telemarketers to sell over the telephone. And the script was designed to work on every single objective. That is what sales is, to overcome the objective and get the order. She would confess, 'I think I may be pregnant', and this telemarketer, so called counselor, would say, 'We can take care of your problem, no one needs to know.' Then the first question on the script is what is the last date of your normal period? She figures that date and gives it to the so-called counselor who puts it on a wheel that is actually designed to calculate the birthdate of the baby, but she didn't talk about birthdate or baby, she says, 'You're eight weeks pregnant.'

"Now what did she do? She confirms this young one's worst fear. I am pregnant. You would think that she would say, 'Stop, how can you tell me I'm pregnant over the telephone?' But this is the pregnancy expert. That seed is planted. That fear is confirmed, and the next question is, 'Is this good news or bad news?' If it were good news, she would not be calling an abortion clinic. If she replies, 'Its bad news' we can go right back in with, 'We can take care of your problem, no one needs to know.' Now she is identifying her fear. Why does she need to know that fear? Because she is going to use it to reaffirm that abortion decision for that young lady.

"The abortions in this nation cost from $300.00 to $12,000.00, advertised. That's because abortions are done through all nine months of pregnancy, not because of Roe vs Wade, it's because of Doe vs Bolton that states, 'for the health of the mother,' it can be completed through all nine months of pregnancy. The problem is, the abortion industry had a different definition for health than we do. Health to the abortion industry includes mental health, so we would say to this scared woman, 'You would have problems with this pregnancy if you carried to term, wouldn't you?' She would say, 'Yes,' and we would chart it as emotional health anxiety.

"The biggest baby I held at 32 weeks, that baby could have lived outside its mother. On the day they come into the abortion clinic, they do the big baby abortions first. Now why do they do that? That woman that has a second or third trimester abortion must stay in recovery longer, she loses more fluid, more blood, she needs a longer period of recovery. And you certainly don't want to be paying a nurse to stay after hours to take care of one or two patients, so you do those first and get them into recovery.

"There are only certain abortionists that do second or third trimester abortions. They come in, they bring the girl in, he can do three of those an hour. But, in the second or third trimester his fee can be up to half of the total cost. So, let's say that $4,000.00 abortion that they are doing in Dallas and Atlanta, he pockets $2,000.00, three an hour, he pockets $6,000.00.

"That's not bad money. But we all know that less than 90% of abortions are first trimester abortions so he can't make that much money doing a $300.00 abortion. That's way too low. But let's make the math easy and let's talk about some numbers.

"We had a technique that we set up to help each abortionist do 10 to 12 an hour. We used two teams of two assistants for each abortionist. The first team would set up the first girl, and he would go in and do that abortion. While across the hall team number two would set up girl number two. Now when he finished that first abortion he ran across the hall. He didn't stop to do operative notes, or surgical scrub, he ran across the hall to room number two, put on fresh gloves, and did abortion number two. Now room number two had to be cleaned, they had to get that girl out and get that room cleaned enough to bring girl number three in so when he finished abortion number two, he could run across the hall and do abortion number three.

"Using that technique an abortionist could do 10 to 12 an hour. Let's say $300.00, he makes a third of the fee for the first trimester, $100.00 for 10 to 12 procedures, $1,000.00 to $1,200.00 per hour. That's not bad money either. But they have added benefits that you and I don't have. You see we did not want to be responsible for any portion of our malpractice insurance. They were independent contractors, not our employees, they collected their money out of one set of books and our money out of another set of books.

"On a busy day we did not know which abortionist would do which abortion. We had two or three working at a time so there was merely a receipt on each chart, and they would collect them and at the end of the day, they would bring them up, give them to the bookkeeper, they would balance them and pay them in cash. No 1099 nor W2. It was left entirely to the discretion of that person to report to the IRS but I'm sure people killing babies for a living report everything, don't you think?"

Do you see how they created literally an assembly line? We're not talking baking pies. We're talking murdering children as fast as you can, for what? Money. It has nothing to do with social rights, you have no rights, there are no rights to kill anybody. Men, women, I don't care, you have no right to choose to kill a child. They turned it into an assembly line to make money. Why? What does the scripture say? The love of money is the root of all kinds of evil. People who want to get rich, a millionaire like that lady. Oh, that's a trap. You are going to start doing some horrible things. I'm telling you, that is what is going on with the abortion industry.

Now that's only half the story. That's only half of how they make their money. As you saw, some of their procedures cost $12,000.00. Especially the later that the baby is in the womb. But the other half is what they do is, they not only make money killing the babies, they also make money off selling the baby parts. This is a well-established fact. It's not some conspiracy. This is well established. They are making money off baby parts. They literally sell each piece of the baby for money. Big money. *"Republicans on the special House Panel investigating the transfer of,* (every time I see the word fetal, I am going to put the appropriate word in there, tissue from murdered babies), *will present evidence in a hearing today that breaks down the price per body part. With release of this evidence, Republicans say they have enough documentation to show that several abortion clinics and middleman procurement businesses may have violated Federal Law.* Because it is against the law. But they still do it for the money. The article shares, and this is not doctored or photoshopped, they literally demonstrate how they itemize the baby. The first one is the baby brains. You can get as much as $3340.00 for a baby's brain.

The baby tissue, again we will see in the next chapter, that if they can't suck it out, when the baby is further developed, they can't just suck it out, they use these things and just start ripping the limbs off. It's sick, but this is literally what is going on. So, you end up with a lot of parts. If you get 10 parts together, you get a bundle deal for almost $6,000.00. You get upper or lower limbs with hands and feet and they will pay you almost $1,000.00. You can get the skull, but it has to match the body parts from the same baby for $595.00. This makes me want to throw up. They literally have this just like going into a restaurant and ordering steak or something, which part of the cow do you want? This is a baby! They tell you that if you can get 38 baby brains together you can get over $22,000.00. This is big business. It's not just the abortion, it's what they do with the body parts. You get 5 baby livers, it's almost $3,000.00, if you get 3 upper and lower limbs, $2,700.00. If you get 12 baby hearts you get over $7,000.00, or 12 baby pancreases and they pay you the same amount of cash. For one baby.

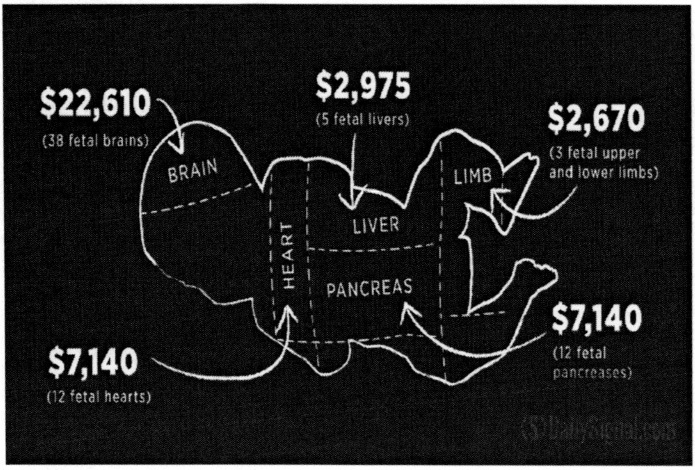

These people are becoming millionaires, it's sick. Now listen to this. Republican Marsha Blackburn, from Tennessee says, in her words, *"It is just horrifying."* And I would agree. She says, *"They are putting a dollar value on the organs of these children, unborn children, that have been murdered. It's just beyond belief."* But, guess who's going to bat for this procedure? The Democrats! Some people say 'Demon-crats.' As you can see, especially with them supporting this, it's getting worse. Oh, and by the way I hear where some Republicans are supporting this. I don't care who you are. If you're a Christian, how in the world could you vote for anybody that supports this? I don't care what party you are from. Shame on you! But you are seeing, by and large, that the Democrat party, I'm starting to call them the 'Death Party', is supporting this. And why would they do that? Money. I'll demonstrate that in a second. The article goes on to say the Democrats on the panel called the investigation a witch hunt by the Republicans that oppose killing babies. Democrats have also condemned the panel investigators for requesting the names of doctors, medical students, researchers, and others involved in the murders and the baby tissue procurement industry. Arguing that if they get the names of these people it could result in the physical harm of these people. Does anyone see the sick irony of that? You are for murdering children and selling their body parts, but you don't want the names released because those people might be physically harmed. It's gross. It's sick. It's what's going on. The sale of services in the acquisition of body parts exploded after President Clinton, a Democrat, signed the National Institute of Health Revitalization Act of 1993. This affected the lifting of the moratorium of funding the research involving baby tissue, or baby parts. So that's sick. That's how they make their money. The love of money is the root of all kinds of evil.

Now, why are they paying so much for this? What do they do with this stuff? We'll find out about that in a second. The distribution of baby body parts to scientists is a million-dollar industry. Researchers say it's a necessary evil, but others say it encourages other abuses. Scientists depend on human body parts, i.e., baby body parts, for research. They believe that it might yield a breakthrough in a number of diseases such as Parkinson's or Alzheimer's. Now you know why they want the brains. Now wait a second. How is that any different of a rationale than what Hitler did to the Jewish people? To not only murder them outside the womb, but abortion is the same thing, they are murdering people inside the womb. But what else did Hitler also do to the Jewish people? He did medical experiments on them. What was his rationale? For the betterment of humanity, of course, the German people, the Nazi's. How is this any different? This is not a slippery slope, there is nothing slippery about this. It's the same mindset. How any Christian can not only vote for people that do this, but to say that it's okay because it's going to help other people down the road. No, murder is wrong. You don't murder somebody to help somebody. It's still murder, and it's still wrong. And again, this is the justification that Hitler used as well. Now, they say they are going to cure diseases but it's still wrong. But they are also using it in vaccinations and it's not only in vaccination development, they actually put baby parts in the vaccinations. It's sick and people are actually being shot up with baby parts. You think it's crazy? Here's one doctor that admitted it.

Interviewer: *"This study involved 74 fetuses?"*

Stanley Plotkin MD: *"76"*

Interviewer: *"And these fetuses were all 3-month fetuses when aborted, correct?"*

Stanley Plotkin MD: *"Yes"*

Interviewer: *"What organs were harvested from these fetuses?"*

Stanley Plotkin, MD: *"I didn't personally harvest any but a whole range of tissues were harvested by co-workers."*

Interviewer: *"And these pieces were cut up into little pieces, right?"*

Stanley Plotkin, MD: *"Right."*

Interviewer: *"They were cultured?"*

Stanley Plotkin, MD: *"Yes."*

Interviewer: *"Some of the pieces were pieces of the pituitary gland, that were chopped up into pieces?"*

Stanley Plotkin, MD: *"Yes."*

Interviewer: *"The lung of the fetus?"*

Stanley Plotkin, MD: *"Yes."*

Interviewer: *"It included kidney, spleen, skin, heart?"*

Stanley Plotkin, MD: *"Yes*

Interviewer: *"And tongue?"*

Stanley Plotkin. MD: *"I don't recall, but probably yes."*

Interviewer: *"Are you aware that one of the vaccinations by the plaintiff in this case inclusion of the aborted fetal tissue, in the development of vaccines and that it actually is part of the ingredients of that vaccine?"*

Stanley Plotkin MD: *"Yes*

Not just the development, it's what? Inside. I don't know if you have been paying attention, but the vaccination issue is becoming a big issue. They say it contains mercury, which is a poison by the way, but there's other issues going on there too. It's gross, it's crazy. Now it goes even beyond that. They are actually using baby body parts to test artificial flavors, spices, seasoning, coffee flavoring, instant soup, bouillon cubes, catsup, sauces and instant noodles. Some of the companies that have been caught doing this are Kraft, Campbell's soup and Pepsi. They say this has only been done in the research and that the actual baby body parts aren't in their food products. But there is a whole debate on this. They deny it but others say no, it's in there too, just like the vaccines. Another thing they do admit that baby parts are also in, it's not just in the vaccines, and this is really sick, Anti-aging skin cream. They admit there are baby parts in there. In gels, serum, and restorative skin cream. You're smearing baby parts on your face so you can look young. You wonder why the wrath of God is coming for 7 years non-stop? Well, we're not done. Now this is a quote from a bioethicist from Boston. He says this. *"They won't be really happy when this is all out in the public. This threatens their business."* So, this again has nothing to do with the woman's right to choose. Nobody has the right to murder a child. It's not even about the woman. If we have a billion-dollar assembly line, money making machine, don't you dare mess with it. We not only make a million dollars from killing babies, we make millions off of their body parts. In fact, one abortionist admitted that she wants to get enough money to buy herself a Lamborghini, by murdering children.

Ezra Levant, The Rebel: *"Another shocking videotape by reporters going undercover with a hidden camera showing Planned Parenthood selling baby body parts as a revenue stream. That's illegal in the United States. But more importantly, it's immoral. Last week I showed you some clips from the first undercover video of the senior executive and doctor at Planned Parenthood talking about buying and selling aborted baby organs while she was stuffing her face at lunch and swirling wine. Seriously, you and I would be nauseous just thinking about such a thing. It was giving her a real appetite, hear this clip from the first video.*

Doctor Nucatola: *"You know, I would throw a number out, I would say it's probably anywhere from $10 to $100 per specimen, depending on the facility and what's involved.*

Buyer/Interviewer: *"The $30 to $100 price range, that's per specimen that we're talking about, right?"*

Doctor Nucatola: *"Per specimen. Yes."*

Ezra Levant: *"But first, let me give you some background. Planned Parenthood is a multi-national corporation that does abortions. They are especially active in aborting minorities. Which is in keeping with the ideology of their corporate founder, Margaret Sanger, who believed in Eugenics, that is, in culling the gene pool of undesirable people. She even started something called the Negro Project. That is what it is called. Specifically designed to abort black babies. That was in the 1930's and early 1940's when getting rid of sub-human races was the global political faction. After WWII with Hitler, the Nazi's, and the Holocaust it became a little bit less fashionable.*

Then there was the whole Black Civil Rights Movement. Margaret Sanger was a racist. So, in 2015, you might think the Eugenics Program was long gone, but it's not. In New York, where Planned Parenthood has its headquarters, according to city health records more black babies are aborted each year than are born alive. 24,000 black babies were born a year in New York while 29,000 black babies were aborted that year in New York. Margaret Sangers' Negro Project is working quite well. And it's also a million-dollar franchise.

It really is a franchise like McDonalds. Planned Parenthood has 800 abortion stores across the United States and some in Canada too. It's not as big as McDonalds which has 14,000 stores in the U.S., but Planned Parenthood is literally a billion dollar a year corporation. Of course, good businesspeople are always looking for ways to make cash. They are also getting cash from women paying for abortions. They also get cash from the government paying for abortions. They make money from the Planned Parenthood Store where they sell shirts and hats for people that are thrilled about abortions. If you're wearing shirts or hats or coffee mugs boasting about abortions, you're not pro-choice anymore. Pro-abortion is different. Pro-choice people say abortions should be safe, legal and rare. That's a phrase I hear a lot. Planned Parenthood wouldn't be a billion-dollar a year franchise though, if abortions were rare. I mean businesses like to grow. Especially enthusiastic business that love what they do. What's so gross here is that The Planned Parenthood abortion store sells baby items too.

It's so gross. They like making money selling abortions and selling abortion apparel. So, it dawned on these abortion entrepreneurs to sell the baby parts themselves. Why throw out the discarded baby parts, why not just sell them for cash. How sick is that? So that is what Dr. Nucatola was talking about last week and now here's another video by another Planned Parenthood executive/doctor, Mary Gaither.

Again, she's not a junior manager, she is a top executive. She's the president of the medical director's council and here she is haggling over prices of baby parts *with these reporters, posing as buyers. She's haggling $70.00 for a baby arm, $100.00 for a baby heart. I mean Planned Parenthood brags that they abort 300,000 babies a year, that is 1,000 per day. Each baby could have 5, 10 organs to sell. We are talking 10's of millions of dollars a year. And this doctor wants to buy a Lamborghini.*

Buyer: "*Now here's another thought, we could talk about specimen, as per specimen, per case, or per procured tissue sample. Which would it be, if we're able to get a liver-thymus pair, you know, it's maybe $75.00 per specimen? So, that's for you, for a liver-thymus pair, that's $150, versus if we can get liver-thymus, brain hemisphere, and all that. So that, that protects us so that we're not paying for what we can't use. And also, I think it also illustrates things for you.*"

Doctor Mary Gatter: "*It's been years since I've talked about compensation, so let me just figure out what others are getting. If this is the ballpark, then it's fine, if it's still low, then we can bump it up. I want a Lamborghini.*" *And she giggles.*

Buyer: "*What did you say?*"

Doctor Mary Gatter: *"I said I want a Lamborghini."*

Abortion, selling baby body parts. What does the scripture say? What was our opening text? The love of money is the root of all kinds of evil. It's sick! Now I don't know if you saw the last Presidential address. That was encouraging that our President would come out and speak against this, but at the end of this video clip, notice who was sitting there and refused to stand.

President Trump: "*There can be no greater contrast to the beautiful image of a mother holding her infant child than the chilling displays our nation saw in recent days. Lawmakers in New York cheered in delight with the passage of legislation that would allow a baby to be ripped from the mother's womb moments from birth. These are living, feeling, beautiful babies who will never get the chance to share their love and their dreams with the world. And then we have the case of the governor of Virginia where he stated that he would execute a baby after birth. To the dignity of every person I am asking Congress to pass legislation to prohibit the late term abortion of children....*"

Republicans cheered in favor of this legislation. But the Democrat side all dressed in black sat in their seats and were silent. As all the cheering and clapping was going on the camera panned to Nancy Pelosi as she sat still in her chair, no cheering, no clapping.

President Trump: *"Who can feel pain in their mother's womb. Let us reaffirm a fundamental truth that all children, born and unborn, are made in the Holy image of God."*

At least it's a start. It would be nice if there were no abortions, no murdering of children, but at least it's a start. But what's so disheartening, no, what's so sickening, you couldn't stand for that? You literally sat there, refused to stand, when he's talking about not murdering children. What's going on in our country right now? It's a spiritual battle. That's insane. Who would basically sit there, and by sitting there, voice your support of murdering children? But again, if you understand the Democrat Party, this has been going on for a long time. And again, I think I know why. Because the abortion industry is a corporation. It's a billion-dollar corporation. We know that politicians will sell out to corporations. They sold out to big pharma. They sold out to the big construction companies. They are paying the lobbyists. Planned Parenthood is a multi-million-dollar corporation and I think that is why you will see Democrats steadfastly support this because somebody's palms are being greased. Somebody is being paid off and this is nothing new. This has been going on for quite some time. Starting with Obama and him having the audacity to say, "God bless Planned Parenthood."

Obama speaking at the Planned Parenthood Gala: *"That's why no matter how great the challenge or how fierce the opposition, there's one thing that the past few years have shown is that Planned Parenthood is not going anywhere. It's not going anywhere today; it's not going anywhere tomorrow." He gets cheers and applause from the crowd. He continues, "As long as we've got to fight to make sure women have access to quality, affordable health care, as long as we've got to fight to make sure that women have the right to make their own choices about her own health, I want you to know that you also have a president whose going to be right there with you, fighting every step of the way. Thank you, Planned Parenthood, God bless you."*

Lauren Ashburn at EWTN News Nightly: *"State leaders have expressed their disappointment and outrage of the passage of the bill in New York that makes abortion legal up until the birth;"*

ABC 9 reports: *"The bill was first introduced in 2007 and removed abortion from the state criminal code and ensures women the right to an abortion in New York if that Federal law should be changed in the Supreme Court. But Cuomo thinks it should be taken a step further."*

Cuomo: *"Make a Constitutional Amendment so that no governor or legislator or political swing can ever jeopardize a woman's right to control her own body in this state."*

Hillary Clinton: *"Far too many women are still denied critical access to reproductive health care and safe childbirth. All the laws we have passed don't count for much if they are not enforced. Rights have to exist in practice not just on paper. Laws have to be backed up with resources and political will and deep-seated cultural codes, religious beliefs and structural biases have to be changed."*

Chelsea Clinton: *"As a deeply religious person, it is also unchristian."*

Chelsea Clinton thinks abolishing abortion is 'unchristian.'

SiriusXM radio reports: *"Whenever we talk about Roe, we are talking about a fight that has been fought through the entirety of our lives. My mother had a bad fight, my grandmother had the fight. How can you have the generational exhaustion?"*

Chelsea Clinton: *"When I think about all of the statistics that are painful, of what women are confronting today, in our country, and what women confronted pre-Roe vs Wade and how many women died and how many more women were maimed because of unsafe abortion practices, we just can't go back to that. That is unconscionable to me, and also, I'm sure this will unleash another wave of hate in my direction, but as a deeply religious person, it is also unchristian."*

Unchristian? Wow! How can people say this? They are grown adults. You ask God to bless Planned Parenthood, you applaud a bill that gives you the right to kill babies right up until birth, you vote against a bill that says babies survive after birth, you say no, the Christians need to change their beliefs on this and you say it's unchristian to not support the murder of children. Why? Well, I've got a theory and it goes like this. Somebody is making a lot of money off this. I think there is certainly accountability, they are just choosing evil and the

Bible says in the last days wickedness is going to rise on an exponential scale and the love of many will grow cold. I think we are certainly in those days. But I do think that a lot of this has to do with this party, the Democrat party is selling out to a big million-dollar corporation. They are the ones helping to keep the assembly lines going so they can buy the Lamborghinis and become millionaires. But it's babies and baby parts. Now in the next chapter we are going to deal with that abortion lady that talked about the assembly line procedure that they made to become millionaires. Believe it or not, we are going to see how she actually considered herself a Christian. She boasts that she tithed on the money she made from killing children. But she was confronted by a real Christian and she got saved. So, we are going to see, how's the church doing on this issue? How are we doing? Are we speaking up? It's not only that we are not speaking up and avoiding this issue but there are churches who have promoted it. Not the world, the church.

Chapter Three

The Church &Abortion

In this chapter we are going to deal with the church. Where is the church in all this when it comes to the issue of abortion? Unfortunately, it's not good news but we need to deal with it. What should we be doing in response and what are our so-called brothers and sisters in Christ doing in response to this mass murder of children? The text we need to look at is 2 Corinthians, Chapter 6. God tells us clearly what we should be doing when it comes to this issue. There's no need to hesitate, there's no need to waffle, there's no need to just sit there and say, 'I need to pray about this,' or 'I need to do some more studying about this.' No, you don't, it's black and white. What you're talking about is murder. And you can't mix the two.

2 Corinthians 6:14-18: *Do not be yoked....*

Now what does the word yoke mean? Joined together. If you were raised in the Midwest, around cows and farming, you know there was this low-tech harness on the cow or ox, you put a couple of them together. It would attach both of their necks so that they would both go at the same time while pulling the plow. It was a yoke that you put on them. That is the word that is used here. In fact, the prefix of this Greek word that means to yoke, not just together, the word used is 'heteros' and it means heterosexual, it means a different kind, if it were the same kind it would be 'homos' or homosexual. So, this is 'heteros', don't yoke yourself with somebody of a completely different kind, and that is the thrust of what he goes into. These people are not Christians. These people are not like us.

So, what do we do? Yes, we witness to anybody on the planet. But we are not talking about witnessing, we're not talking about reaching that lost person, we are talking about yoking yourself together with something of a completely different kind. And that would most definitely be those that would promote the mass murder of children.

...together with unbelievers.

Don't be yoked together with who? He spells it out, unbelievers. Then He gives you several different examples in case you don't get that obvious statement.

...For what do righteousness and wickedness have in common?

We would use the term today, oil and water, it doesn't mix.

...Or what fellowship can light have with darkness? What harmony...

Isn't that what the ecumenical movement is saying today, we must all work together, forget truth, we just love, love, love, we just have harmony?

...is there between Christ and Belial?

Belial is basically, in scripture, satan. Are you actually going to try to combine Christ with satan? What are you doing here?

...What does a believer have in common with an unbeliever? What agreement is there between the temple of God and idols?...

Did you know that the love of money is an idol? But what are these people doing? They want to get rich. That's their idol, that's their god.

...For we are the temple of the living God. As God has said: "I will live with them and walk among them, and I will be their God and they will be my people."

We just need to let the people know we love them, don't talk about the truth, don't mention that because then they might leave. We are just going to dance around the issue and act all happy and then somehow that's going to be great. Wrong! What does God say? Get out of there! Again, we aren't talking about witnessing, we're talking about being yoked.

...Therefore, come out from them and be separate, says the Lord. Touch no unclean thing, and I will receive you. I will be a Father to you, and you will be my sons and daughters, says the Lord Almighty.

So that is what we are going to see in this chapter, the theme is, what I think is obvious when it comes to God's word, this issue is cut and dried, black and white, abortion is the mass murder of children and what is God's response to that evil? The darkness. We are working with Belial or satan. What should we do? Should we work together on it? Should we compromise on it? No, and that is what we are going to see further into this chapter. Unfortunately, that is what the church is doing. We are going to start off with part 3 of our video, *The Voice of John.* You are also going to see the abortion provider that claimed to be a Christian.

Carol Everett: *"We had two abortion clinics open and we opened three more to meet my goal and become a millionaire. An abortion clinic can open one day and pay for itself in the first month and be a cash cow the second month. Our goal was to open three more abortion clinics in the next year. Now everybody in the abortion clinic fights. The counselors fight, the nurses fight, the managers fight.*

"It was the doctor and his live-in girlfriend and me. We, the girlfriend and I had great difficulty, so we called in a man that was introduced to us as a business counselor who said he could solve our problems by merely meeting with the three of us an hour a week for 4 weeks. So, you have probably figured that I can talk to anybody for four hours so that wasn't a problem. To me, I was going to be a millionaire next year.

"He was a very strange man. He would not talk about money. He wouldn't talk about how much he would charge. I didn't care, I was going to be a millionaire. And we started meeting with him. The second time I sat down with him I noticed something so very different about him. I couldn't understand it. He didn't fit into my world. He didn't drink, he didn't cuss, he didn't smoke, he didn't run out on his wife, he didn't do drugs, and I don't know why to this day, but I asked him, 'Are you a preacher?' He said, 'Yes.'

"I asked, 'Why in the world are you in this situation?' He said, 'God sent me.' I knew the man was crazy. I said, 'I'm a Christian. I have a Bible in the top right-hand drawer of my desk. I will have you know that I pray every day.' I didn't tell him that I prayed that none of those women would die from the abortions today.

"But I told him that I tithed on all that money and he was not impressed. I had a sick feeling in the pit of my stomach that I was in trouble. He said, 'Carol, my deacons and I have been praying that there is someone inside this abortion clinic that God wants out.' He said, 'We are going to be leaving in thirty days.' I was pretty excited. I had already picked out the person that he could take with him when he left. But he didn't stop there. He said, 'Carol, God loves you! He loves you and He knows that you can't work hard enough, you can't be good enough, Carol, you can't buy your way to Heaven.

"But because God loves you so much, he made a way of escape for you. He sent His son to walk the face of the earth to live that sin-free life and die on the cross in that perfect sacrifice for your sin. And by the simple act of faith in Jesus Christ as your savior and Lord, your life can change.' He said, 'I wouldn't be much of a salesman if I didn't ask you to pray that simple prayer and ask Jesus Christ to come into your life and into your heart.' I've been a deal maker all my life and that was such a simple deal. I actually thought I'd pray that simple prayer and shut that man up.

"But he was and is the king of the word prayer. He said, 'Carol, I'm going to pray this prayer and you say it after me.' And the prayer he prayed is this. 'Dear God, I am a sinner. Please forgive me of my sins. Thank you for sending your son, Jesus Christ, to die on the cross for my sins. Reign on my heart as Lord and Savior. Make me a worker in your vineyard. Amen.' I got up, I shook his hand, I said good-bye, I got in my car, and I laughed all the way back to that abortion clinic.

"When I got back to that abortion clinic something had happened. Those girls were all huddled over in the corner and they were all crying. I'd never seen that before. I'm sure it happened. I started taking them back to my office and sitting down with them, eye to eye, knee to knee, saying, 'You don't have to have an abortion. Your parents will not kill you. Just go home, I'll go home with you and talk to them.' At the end of that day I could say I saved three babies today, I lost $75.00. I had two kids in college. Money, money, money. That's where my heart was.

"And I fell to my knees on the floor of that abortion clinic and a few hours after the first prayer, I prayed a heart prayer. 'Lord, if there is a Lord, if this is not where you want me, hit me over the head with a two by four.' I did not know that He had one, but he did, and it was very swift. Our clinics were caught by the CBS

affiliate in Dallas, Texas at that time. Attempting to do abortions at that time who were not pregnant. They sent the reporter to the doctor to be certain that they were not pregnant and then they were sent to our clinic wired for sound and caught us red handed saying 'yep you're pregnant', we just want your money, let's do it now. It was just 27 days since that pastor said that someone would be leaving in 30 days and all along it was me."

Melissa Ohden: *"I think that when most people hear about abortion survivors around the world they automatically think a woman and sometimes a man who have experienced an abortion in their life and have suffered the consequences as a result of that and what people don't often think about is that the word abortion survivor actually describes a group of people who have survived their own abortions.*

"And I know that because I'm one of them. I don't think that people recognize when they first see me that I suffered what I did when I was just an infant. My birth mother had a saline induced abortion and she thought she was less than five months pregnant when she went in to have that abortion. And what that actually entailed was a toxic salt solution being delivered into the amniotic fluid surrounding me in the womb.

"The intent of that salt solution was to scald me to death. And as people look up saline infusion abortions in medical journals or you look it up online, you'll read about how that toxic salt solution is meant to scald the child. It burns the skin, peels it away, moves internally into the organs to literally burn the child to death and that type of procedure typically takes place over about three days. What I know, in the case of my biological mothers' abortion and my life, is that I soaked in that toxic salt solution for five days.

"And I tell people I can't imagine what it was like for me to have to fight for my life in the womb because of what that procedure involves, is the child fighting and the woman feeling the child thrashing around in the womb, fighting for their life. So, not only can I not imagine what it was like for me, but I can't imagine what it was like for my biological mother to have that salt solution delivered, to go home and wait for the sign that the life inside of her had been effectively snuffed out.

"Then to go back to the hospital on the fifth day and have her premature labor induced in the hopes that she would deliver a dead child that day. I can't

imagine. But what I do know is that when she went back to the hospital on the fifth day, at St. Luke's Hospital in Sioux City, Iowa, her labor was induced with me and I was delivered. I was initially believed to be a successful abortion.

"From what my adoptive parents were told, they cast me aside, left me for dead in my mothers' hospital room, while they tended to her, they were going to dispose of me later. Now I know this is my life, but sometimes I can't imagine what the beginning of my life was truly like. When I survived that day and I was initially left for dead, and I was laid aside, God had other plans that day.

"That's what brings me great joy, that in spite of how I was left in that hospital room, God allowed me the opportunity to make weak grunting noises and tiny movements with my little body and there was that nurse still tending to my biological mother and that was when they realized that the abortion had not succeeded in ending my life. That is when the medical procedures began that sustained my life. I always tell people that I know, by looking at me, people find it hard to imagine. But God does miraculous things."

Even in the midst of such horrific behavior, wow! Black and white, isn't it? How could anyone even hesitate on this issue. But that's what's happening. It's not just the hesitation, the more I got into the research for this study, it blew me away. I knew it was bad, but I didn't realize it was this bad. I'm not talking the world, we already dealt with that in the last two chapters. I'm talking about the church. But my theory is, we are still back to Romans 1. Because once you make that first compromise and you buy into that lie of evolution and have the audacity to say that God doesn't exist, then you start compromising on sexual immorality, then comes homosexuality, and then you do things that ought not be done, like abortion, the mass murder of children. Now we look at that, we deal with that context in the world, but what's going on in the church? Is the church compromising on evolution? How many churches do you know that have even done a study on evolution vs creation, let alone support a literal six-day creation Genesis account? Rare to none. You think prophecy is bad? That's just as bad. The church is not dealing with that. Some churches are even promoting evolution if you can believe that. They are even doing Darwin Sundays. So, the church has already done that. Is the church sliding on that, on immorality? It's all over the place. To the point that I can't believe I still have to have discussions with people that it's wrong to live together, let alone have sex outside of marriage, which is fornication by the way. Which leads to, now we have to commit murder for that mistake. Right? So, is the church sliding on homosexuality? Yes, you see it's following the same thread of Romans l as the world is. What does darkness have with light? Christ with Belial? Are you trying to mix the two? No way! Don't be yoked! It's bad! I need to show you a couple examples of churches. Not just churches, but clergy supporting abortion. This was recently. Religious leaders bless the opening of Planned Parenthood, a new abortion clinic, and they call it a sacred work. Here is the picture. There are a bunch of them.

They admit, *"Blessing an abortion clinic may seem antithetical to religious beliefs about the sanctity of life but, various religious leaders did that on Tuesday at Planned Parenthood's newest abortion clinic, (*mass murder of children facility*), in Washington, D.C. Religious leaders representing more than 20 churches participated in the ceremony inside the new mega-facility."*

So, these guys have really got the assembly line going. The new abortion facility is located next to Two Rivers Public Charter School. And from what we saw, that is why they are putting sex-ed in the schools. To what? To get them sexually active so they can become a customer. They admitted that. This is from the CEO**, Dr. Laura Meyers**, of Planned Parenthood, in metropolitan Washington, with this so-called clergy support, listen to what her response is:

"In almost every message to our staff I talk about doing our sacred work. This, (the so-called clergy involvement and blessing) *confirms the sacredness of the work we do."* (Of mass murdering of children.) Later she said, *"Pro-lifers tried to separate those of us working on or supporting the right of women to choose, from a deep sense of spirituality. So today it's a shift in that narrative."*

In other words, they are joining forces with us. People supposedly being Christians. I'm not talking about the world, but they are supposed to be Christians, and Christian leaders. Now listen to this, before the ceremony kicked off, religious leaders went upstairs to have a prayer circle. It was like an ecumenical thing. It was led by Rabbi Michael Namath. He called upon the obligation of the world to make it whole and Holy. Through abortion? Now the irony of this statement is that this is a Jewish Rabbi, this is Eugenics, this is what Hitler did to the Jewish people, and now he is supporting this and saying we are going to make the world whole and Holy. That's what Hitler thought he was doing. Exterminating people to create his master race. That's kind of ironic. Then the formal event began, featuring people from different Christian denominations. Then it was joined by Hindu priests, Muslim imams, and they did visual art and liturgical dance. Because you have to act religious. Listen to what this guy had to say.

Willie Parker: *"I've been a Christian longer than I have been an abortion provider."*

Do you see the oxymoron? Like icy hot, peaceful war, it doesn't mix, it doesn't work. What? You have been a Christian longer than you have been an abortion provider? He said...

"Women have been made to believe that this clinic is some evil place where God is not. Cursing women for making sacred decisions. Our answer to the curse is to bless us, Planned Parenthood. "Then the medical director of Planned Parenthood said she plans to tell patients that *"the abortion facility is now a blessed space and that those of faith support your decision."*

And ended by singing 'This Little Light of Mine.' Christians, supposed Christians, key word, supposed. That's one example. Then here is this guy. He is a Charismatic, Word of Faith. That is a lie, it's Hinduism. We saw that in our Charismatic study. But he is a fellow evangelist and he is urging people in his church to not just get vasectomies, but to get abortions. His name is Ernest Angley. And the Akron Beacon Journal in Ohio did an investigation on him and found out that, in fact, he not only encourages men to have vasectomies, but for them to not have children and to again, encourage abortions. You know why? Listen to this, remember he is Word of Faith. It's all about money,

wealth, he says, *"He doesn't want people to have kids because it would take time and money away from the church."* Because what is he all about? Money. Other church officials said, "he was a liar, a drug addict and an adulterer." And he wouldn't respond to the Beacon. Then, he claims to be a prophet of God and he can heal people of their afflictions. Do you see another irony there? You're supposed to be a prophet of God, speaking for God, which is not true, but God doesn't support this, and then you say you have the gift to heal people of their afflictions, but you encourage them to murder children. This is in the church, not just in the world.

Let me give you another example. A Presbyterian minister blesses Planned Parenthood clinic and he serves as their pastor. Marvin Ellison is in Portland where he "blesses the operation with prayer" and he wrote the following.

Marvin Ellison: *"We are proud to be part of the highly professional and highly caring health care team."* No, you are a death squad! He said as chaplain, *"We undertake this work not in spite of but because of our faith and values."* What do you mean faith and values? What Bible are you reading? Then he has the audacity to say this: *"It's his belief in the Bible that leads him to work for Planned Parenthood and not against them. In fact, God is absolutely for abortion."* He goes on to say, *"As a minister he is to give women spiritual permission to kill their unborn child."*

Every woman that has had an abortion, and we haven't got to that part yet, say that they know that this is wrong. Because you have a conscience that God gave you and then here is this guy that is supposed to be a pastor and he is helping them to remove that sting of conviction. Then he goes on to say this ...

Marvin Ellison: *"We thank God for Planned Parenthood and for the amazing work you do."*

Isaiah 5:20: "Woe unto those that call evil good and good evil. That put darkness for light and light for darkness. That put bitter for sweet and sweet for bitter."

But he's not the only one. It doesn't really surprise me. I knew it was bad, I knew it was going on, I just didn't realize how bad it was in the church today. But let me give you a couple more examples of so-called Christians blessing Planned Parenthood.

Catherine Szeltner, Host of EWTN Pro-Life Weekly: "*This next story is an example of so-called religious leaders leading their flock astray and twisting God's word to feed an agenda of death and destruction. Based on a Facebook post by 'Whole Woman's Health' and an article in the Texas Observatory earlier this month from so-called clergy gathered at an abortion clinic in Ft Worth, Texas, to quote, 'bless abortion providers, clinic staff, and patients.'*

The group reportedly saying Halleluiah and praise. When we say Halleluiah, we should be praising God and not praising abortion which goes directly against God, the author of life. If we are going to debate abortion on Biblical grounds, it's clear where the Good Book stands. 'Thou shalt not kill,' 'before you were formed in the womb, I knew you,' and many more verses.

It's not up for debate. We condemn an event that twists Christianity to fit an abortion agenda. The Ohio Religious Coalition for Reproductive Choice will host a clinic blessing at an Ohio Planned Parenthood abortion clinic next Friday. Organizers said they want to show that anti-abortion advocates do not have the monopoly on faith or God.

They even claim that, 'many faith leaders and people of faith hold that accessing and providing abortions are good and Godly decisions.' What these so-called religious leaders are doing is dishonest and deceitful. By using ministers and twisting truth to sway the people to support abortion is nothing new for the industry.

In a 1939 letter, Planned Parenthood founder, Margaret Sanger, wrote: "We do not want word to go out that we want to exterminate the negro population and the minister is the man who can straighten out that idea if it ever occurs to any of their more rebellious members.' Just because they put a collar on it doesn't mean it's truth. Be warned my friends this letter is a perversion of faith and these clergy members are false shepherds."

Interesting, I love that line, just because you put a collar on it, it doesn't make it the truth. But hey, if somebody goes to a seminary, does that make them a Christian? If somebody gets behind a pulpit, does that mean they are a Christian? If somebody is an educator and says, God told me to tell you, does that make them a Christian? No, the American church is flooded with so many false shepherd's and false Christians, it has gotten so bad because we don't have a standard. You see, Paul warned over and over again in scripture many different times that these false fakers would come into the church and you need to get them out. You don't need to put up with these false teachers and these false prophets. But we don't have a standard anymore because we aren't preaching the truth. So, it's all about numbers. Anybody can come in and that's been going on for a whole generation now, for at least 25 years, if not more.

It's called the church growth movement. So, anybody that comes up, add them to the list. Well, guess what, those people don't always just sit in the pews, where do they go? Sometimes they get into your Sunday School class, sometimes they serve on your church board, sometimes they are behind your pulpit. My theory is, this has gone on for so long that they are the ones that are controlling the church. I'm talking about Christians. Because how in the world can you just sit there and ask God to bless the mass murder of children and you are really a Christian? Personally, I have a problem with that. No conviction? It isn't that you just don't want to deal with it or support it, something is wrong. Right? But let me give you an example of how far it's gone, it isn't just the so-called clergy supporting it, but again, I'm telling you, the standard is so low today that is allowing this to take place that now there is an increase in our country of what they call atheist churches. Or Godless churches. It looks like a church, you sing and do religious things like a church, but at least these guys don't hide behind a collar or a mask. They admit, no, we're not Christians, we just like to feel religious. It's actually increasing in our country.

Adam Gabbatt of the Guardian: "*Today the Sunday assembly of the atheist church is launching 35 new services across the world. One is in New Zealand, Hungary, France, the UK, and 16 here in the United States. So, I'm here at the one in Strongsville, Ohio, just outside Cleveland and we're going to see what it is all about.*"

He walks into the hall and everyone is seated while a couple of guys are playing guitars and singing their songs. One of the flyers states, 'Live Better. Help often. Wonder more.'

Adam Gabbatt: *"What is your background? Were you raised in a religious family? Did you go to church?"*

Eric Tawney, Sunday Assembly organizer: *"I think I was saved twice. It obviously didn't take. Recently I was just de-baptized. I have the actual certificate showing that I was de-baptized."*

Adam Gabbatt: *"How do you get de-baptized? Do they dry you excessively?"* and they laugh.

The service starts. They all clap and a gentleman steps up to the podium and begins to speak. *"The simple idea we like to spread is that we have one life which means that that life needs to be lived to the fullest. There is no second chance. No opportunity to have a do-over. There is no after-life in which wrongs are righted and cosmic justice handed out to the evil doer."*

Adam Gabbatt: *"The Sunday Assembly was started by two British comedians, Sanderson Jones and Pippa Evans. They held the first event in London in January of 2013. After that, Jones and Evans found that people were getting in touch, asking how they could set up their own Sunday Assembly."*

Adam Gabbatt: *"What was it like and now being a most prominent atheist and organizing something like this? Do you get any push back from people that are religious that you know?"*

Layla Nelson: *"I do know several close friends who are religious. One of my best friends from high school. She is a pastor. I actually turned to my pastor friend and ask her how do you start a church and she gave me reams of advice. Lots of great ideas."*

Adam Gabbatt: *"Your pastor friend gave you advice on how to start a godless church?"*

Layla Nelson: *"Yes."* And they laughed.

Maybe it's because you have more in common than you realize. You shouldn't have a female pastor in the first place. The Bible is very clear about that. It's wrong, it's a godless decision. But then you have this, so-called, female pastor in a godless position, giving godless advice, to start a godless atheist church. This is what is going on in our country. And again, what's going on here? That guy that says I was saved twice but it didn't stick. What are we dealing with here? These are people, in my opinion, scripturally, because that is more important than my opinion, but my opinion based on the scripture, you're not saved. Because you cannot lose your salvation. He may have walked up to the altar, even said a prayer, that doesn't save you. Right? There has to be a genuine conversion. The genuine conversion, you're born again, and the Spirit of God dwells in you, it happens at the moment of salvation, there is no way you can support this

I'll give you a personal example. In my testimony, believe it or not, I was all about rebellion, all about self, don't tell me what to do, don't call me a sinner, right? I was involved in the occult, New Age, the whole nine yards. It was all about self. I was going to do what I wanted to do, and nobody was going to tell me what to do. And believe it or not, even I, as a guy, at that time, supported abortion. Why? Because nobody should tell anybody what to do. It's that rebellious mindset, right? I kid you not, many multitudes of things were going through my brain the moment I got saved, I was crying at the same time, it was absolutely phenomenal. I could feel the weight of the sin being lifted; I was brand new. I shared my testimony the first couple days, the grass was greener, the sky was bluer, but instantly getting saved, I didn't read a verse, nobody preached to me, I didn't watch a video study on it, I instantly knew that abortion was wrong. Why? Because the spirit of God was inside of me now. These aren't people just avoiding the issue, they aren't just waffling on the issue, they don't want to touch the issue, these are the people that say we support it and are asking God to bless it. I'm sorry I don't think you can be a Christian and do that. Now if you think that's wild let's take a look at what the Bible repeatedly says. You might say "Well, maybe that is just some isolated passage." Are you kidding me? The Bible repeatedly warns, especially in the last days, you are going to be surrounded in the church by so many fake people you better keep your eyes open. Let's deal with what the scripture says...

DEAD FAITH BELIEVERS

James 2:14,17 "What good is it, my brothers, if a man claims to have faith but has no deeds? Can such faith save him? In the same way, faith by itself, if it is not accompanied by action, is dead. You believe that there is no God. Even the demons believe that – and shudder."

It's not saying that you are saved by your works, but when you get saved what happens to your insides? The Holy Spirit is inside of you and guess what? Your works change. He convicts you of sin. You're not happy in sin. You're not complacent in sin. I'm not saying you don't sin. I'm saying that your attitude towards sin changed. And you want to serve Jesus. So, he's saying that if you have faith and nothing changes, it's fake. It's called a dead faith. A dead faith is not a saving faith. Are demons going to Heaven? How many people have you heard say I believe in God? I'm a Christian. Really? You're doing no better than demons.

DEAD ATTENDANCE BELIEVERS

1 John 2:19 "They went out from us, but they did not really belong to us. For if they had belonged to us, they would have remained with us; but their going showed that none of them belonged to us."

This answers that guy that said he had got saved twice but it didn't stick. No, you were fake the whole time. The scripture says they were fake. They were fake the whole time. Just like Judas Iscariot. He was right in the midst, but he was fake. I'm telling you this happens on a grander scale and I don't think we even want to deal with.

DEAD RELIGION BELIEVERS

Matthew 7:21-12 "Not everyone who says to me, Lord, Lord, will enter the kingdom of Heaven, but only he who does the will of my Father who is in Heaven. Many will say to me on that day, Lord, Lord, did we not prophesy in your name, and in your name drive out demons and perform many miracles? Then I will tell them plainly, I never knew you. Away from me, you evildoers!"

Those people, they were clapping, singing songs, because they liked being religious. But religion doesn't save you.

DEAD BEHAVIOR BELIEVERS

You claim to be a Christian, but the acid test is in how you live. We're not saved by our works but if nothing changes, you're not fooling anybody but yourself.

Titus 1:16 "Such people claim they know God, but they deny him by the way they live. They are despicable and disobedient, worthless for doing anything good."

FALSE BROTHERS

(Greek-pseudadelphos-a false brother, one who in a showy way professes to be a Christian but is destitute of Christian piety or knowledge.)

They make big claims, look at me, I'm a Christian, I dress like a Christian, I look like a Christian, I act like a Christian, I go to religious things, I try to do Christian religious deeds, and make a big deal of it, but you're not a Christian. Paul gives many examples of these in the church. He says...

Galatians 2:4 "This matter arose because some false brothers had infiltrated our ranks to spy on the freedom we have in Christ Jesus and to make us slaves."

Fake Christians are coming into the church.

2 Corinthians 11:26 "I have been constantly on the move. I have been in danger from rivers, in danger from bandits, in danger from my own countrymen, in danger from Gentiles; in danger in the city, in danger in the country, in danger at sea; and in danger from false brothers."

Who came after him and caused him trouble? Fake Christians. Do you think fake Christians ever give us a ruckus? Do you think we have ever had to deal with that as a church? It has happened at every church I have ever pastored. The church is flooded with fake people because nobody holds the standard, by and large it is so lowered today.

FALSE LEADERS (prophets and teachers)

Matthew 7:15,16 "Watch out for false prophets. They come to you in sheep's clothing, but inwardly they are ferocious wolves. By their fruit you will recognize them."

False prophets, like that guy that said don't have kids, get an abortion, because you need to give me your money. That's what he was doing. He said he was a prophet. If you encourage people to kill children and all you want is their money, I have a problem with that. "Well you are just being intolerant." No, I'm not! Jesus said that by their fruits you are going to recognize them. Now I'm not saying that I'm perfect, because I'm not, but promoting the murder of children, and ripping people off?

2 Corinthians 11:13 "For such men are false apostles, deceitful workmen, masquerading as apostles of Christ."

2 Corinthians 11:14-15 "And no wonder, for satan himself masquerades as an angel of light. It is not surprising, then, if his servants masquerade as servants of righteousness, their end will be what their actions deserve."

His servants masquerade as servants of light, including banding together with other religions and saying we need to come here in a prayer circle and do this art dance and bless murdering children.

2 Peter 2:1 "But there were also false prophets among the people, just as there will be false teachers among you. (Where? What's the context? In the CHURCH!) They will secretly introduce destructive heresies, even denying the sovereign Lord who bought them – bringing swift destruction on themselves. Many will follow their shameful ways and will bring the way of truth into disrepute."

Wow, now maybe you think it is just those liberal churches. The fake Christianity. No, even those who claim to be evangelicals like you and I are going along with this. Let me show you this, from George Barna. In case you're not familiar with him, he does all kinds of statistical data. He talks about Americans/Christians being confused about abortion, which I thought was interesting because what is so confusing about it? It's wrong! But listen to what he said.

"The majority of those who say they are pro-life, even though they say they would not have an abortion, they think that everyone should have the right to choose."

Then you are not pro-life.

"One quarter of the proclaimed pro-lifers believe abortion should be allowed if the baby is less than one month old."

Then you're not pro-life!

"*Of almost one in four pro-lifers, 23% contend that abortion should be legal in most or all circumstances.*"

Then you're not pro-life! And then, on top of that:

"One *fourth of the self-proclaimed pro-choice, 25% admit that abortion is murder.*"

But about the same amount say that it should be legal in most circumstances. Now, these are people who noted on a survey that they are not only a Christian, but a *born-again* Christian. They're not that godless church, they're not the liberal type, they're not the ones that have female pastors, not that type, they are supposed to be *born-again*. First of all, 43% consider themselves strong pro-life. These are people that are supposedly born-again. Why isn't it 100%? It's not even half, it's 43%. Again, I'm not talking liberal, I'm not talking atheist. No, these are the ones who claim to be the real deal, the real born-again Christian.

Now, how many of those who claim to be born-again Christians say that abortions should be legal if the baby is less than one month old? 45% support that. You can kill the child in the first trimester, 32% of those claiming to be born-again Christians said that's okay. In the second trimester, 15% of those claiming to be born-again Christians say that's okay. How many of you, as born-again Christians agree with the stopping of the funding of Planned Parenthood? 30%. Can I flip that around for you? Do the math. Those proclaiming to be born-again Christians, 70%, have no problem with Planned Parenthood continuing to get funding.

But I really want to make it easy for us. Should we really support this? Is there room to waffle on it? Is it really that bad? Yes, it is. And the people in Congress recently met on the Planned Parenthood issue, trying to get rid of the funding, which I hope they do, but at least some people in Congress admit what is really going on when they do an abortion and they mass murder children. This is from the House Judiciary Committee Rayburn Office Building.

Rep. Bob Goodlatte: "*We welcome our distinguished witnesses today. Do each of you swear that the testimony that you are about to give will be the truth, the* *whole truth, and nothing but the truth, so help you God? So, I will introduce to you our first witness Dr. Anthony Levatino. Dr. Levatino is a board-certified gynecologist, obstetrician and over the course of his career Dr. Levatino has practiced obstetrics and gynecology in both private and university settings, including as a professor of OBGYN at the Albany Medical College. And Dr. Levatino we will start with you, welcome."*

Dr. Anthony Levatino: "*Thank you chairman and members of the committee. I only have 5 minutes, so I am going to get right to it. Second trimester D & E abortions performed roughly between 14 and 24 weeks of gestation. Your patient today is 17 years old and she's 22 weeks pregnant. Her baby is the length of your hand plus a couple inches. And she has been feeling her baby kick for the past several weeks.*

"She's asleep on an operating room table. You walk into that operating room scrubbed and gowned. After removing laminaria you introduce the suction catheter into the uterus. This is a 14-inch suction catheter. If she was pregnant 14 weeks or less, the baby is basically the width of your hand or smaller, you could do the entire procedure with this but, babies this big don't fit through catheters this size. After suctioning the amniotic fluid out from around the baby you introduce the instrument called the sofer clamp, it's about 13 inches long and it is made of stainless steel. The business end of this clamp is about 2 1/2 inches long and half inch wide with rows of sharp teeth. This is a grasping instrument. When it gets hold of something it does not let go.

"A D & E procedure is a blind abortion. So, picture yourself introducing it and grabbing anything you can, blindly, and pull and I do mean pull hard and out pops a leg about this big, 5 inches long, and you lay it onto the table next to you. You reach in again and pull again and you pull out an arm about the same length, which you put down on the table next to you. You use this instrument again and again to tear out the spine, the intestines, the heart and lungs.

"The head of the baby of that size is about the size of a large plum. You can't see it, but you have a pretty good idea that you got your instrument around something and your instrument is spread about as far as it goes. You know you did it right if you crush down on it and white material runs out of the mother's cervix, it was the baby's brains, then you can pull out skull pieces. If you have a day like I had a lot of times, sometimes a little face comes back and stares at you.

Congratulations you just performed a second trimester D & E abortion. You just affirmed her right to choose."

Rep. Bob Goodlatte: *"One more question Dr. Levatino, why did you end your practice of performing abortions?"*

Dr. Levatino: *"I did over 1200 abortions over a 4-year period of private practice not counting the ones I did during my training. I met my wife during my first year of training at the Albany Medical Center. We got married about a year later and found we had an infertility problem. After years of infertility treatments and several years of trying to adopt a child we were blessed with being able to adopt a little girl that we named Heather in August of 1978.*

"As sometimes happens in those situations my wife got pregnant the very next month and we had two children 10 months apart. Two months short of my daughter Heathers 6th birthday she was killed in an automobile accident. She literally died in my arms in the back of an ambulance. Anyone who has children might think they have some idea what that feels like but until you have been through it yourself you have no idea whatsoever.

"I know people find it hard to believe but what do you do after a disaster? You bury your child and then you go back to your life. I don't remember exactly how long it was after my daughter died that I showed up at Albany Medical Center OR#9 to perform my first second trimester D & E abortion. I wasn't thinking it was anything special. It was routine to me. But I reached in, literally pulled out an arm or a leg and got sick.

"Earlier on I described stacking body parts on the side of the table, but it's not to gross people out. When you do an abortion, you have to keep an inventory to make sure you have two arms, two legs, and all the pieces. If you don't, your patient is going to come back infected, bleeding, or dead. So, I soldiered on and finished that abortion and I know I said it is hard for people to believe but I am telling you straight up my experience.

"After over 1200 abortions of first and second trimesters, up to 24 weeks, and all the rest of it and being very dedicated to it, for the first time in my life I really looked. I really looked at the pile of body parts that laid on the side of the table and I didn't see her wonderful right to choose, I didn't see all the money I just

made, all I could see was somebody's son or daughter and I stopped doing late term abortions after that. Several months later I stopped doing all abortions."

Rep. Bob Goodlatte: "*Thank you."*

Washington Times: *"Not a single pro-lifer to be found for largest Democratic presidential field in history."*

Man, where is everybody? We should be shouting this from the roof tops. Oh, and by the way, you wonder why I called the Democratic Party the Death Party? Did you catch that last part? Not a single person in the Democratic party is pro-life, and if you vote for that... But maybe that's just us. Maybe it's just our generation, the younger generation coming up, they seem more active. They seem like they want to change the world. Surely, they are taking a stand on this, aren't they? Let me give these stats again. George Barna talks about the millennial age, the generation coming up.

George Barna: "*While there is ample evidence that the millennials and the baby boomers have radically different lifestyles and views of the world, both generations have surprisingly similar views on abortion. Millennials are much more likely to approve of abortions regardless of the age of the baby. They view the decision of the woman's choice as more important than the baby having any rights. The younger group is less likely to view the baby as a human upon conception and they are much less prone to halting the funding to Planned Parenthood and are less likely to describe themselves as pro-life."* That's the generation coming up and getting ready to come into power. And then he explains the confusion. My interpretation, you reap what you sow. We've had 25 plus years of not preaching the word of God and this is what we're left with.

George Barna: *There has been a broad and consistent decline in Christian commitment. (*And not just attending the church services, take it or leave it*) but not reading the Bible, accepting Jesus as their savior. (*We don't need to do that either apparently.) *And even possessing a Biblical world view. (*Who cares what the Bible says, I will decide!) *This is why it is this way."*

He also pointed out that in this generation there is a rise in narcissism, it's all about self. And post modernism, which says that you get to decide what is right and what is wrong.

George Barna: "*How do we get to this place?' Most of conservative churches in the United States of America still refuse to teach people how to think Biblically or even deal with controversial issues and pastors steadfastly refuse to teach or preach on these issues, religious persecution, homosexuality, Israel, you name it, they don't touch it with a 10 ft pole.*"

Why? Because the church growth movement has infected the church! If it's all about numbers and you don't preach the truth because people will leave. When it's the truth that keeps us strong, it's the truth that sets people free, if you don't preach the truth, you got your numbers all right, but are these people even saved? They are on your staff, behind your pulpits, directing the church now and the ones coming up, they are being catered to. The ones that are about self. Don't tell me what is right and wrong. I'll decide. And if you think that the pastors that now 'cater to the millennial generation' are going to turn things around, listen to this. This is Pastor Carl Lentz. He is the pastor of Hillsong, which is one of the biggest millennial churches out there. He had a chance on National TV to stand up for abortion and this is how he did on the View.

The View: "*Hillsong is seen as a hip progressive church with a huge millennial crowd, but it's still evangelical. So where do you stand on social issues that young people are particularly passionate about like gay marriage, abortion. How do you address those issues? So, it's not a sin in your church to have an abortion?*

Pastor Carl Lentz: "*That is the kind of conversation we would have to just find out where you're from, what do you believe in, I mean God's the judge, people have to live with their own convictions. If I have to tell you....(applause)*"

If I have to tell you? What in the world is a pastor supposed to do? I'll tell you right here from the Word of God. It's not that complicated, dude. Yes, it is a sin! Bang, case closed. He would say nothing, and that is one of the big ones. One of the supposed big guys that is out there in the millennial generation. Folks, it's not looking good. Again, I'm not here to be pessimistic but we have to deal with this. We're not responsible for other people's behavior, but we are responsible for our own. So, let's just make sure that we do speak up, in love, and get the truth out. Because it's not just about standing for the truth, as important as that is, God's word is very clear. This is wrong, this is murder. But for every person that we have the privilege to lead to Christ and lead them away from this behavior, this is not just the world ideals that got changed, a life was saved. A baby was rescued. Let's do that with our time.

Chapter Four

The Survivors of Abortion

In this chapter we are going to get into the fourth aspect. We have the history, the motive, the church and now we get into the survivors of abortion, murder attempts in the womb. When we talk about the survivors, it's not the men and women who actually attempted to murder their child, because that is what abortion is, we are talking about the children that survived their own murder attempt. Now stop right there and let that sink in for just a moment. We're talking about children who survived their own murder attempt. That's what we are going to deal with in this chapter. You wonder why the wrath of God is not just coming, you wonder why the wrath of God is coming for 7 years non-stop? Not 7 minutes, not 7 days, not 7 months, but for 7 years, non-stop to this planet? I think the issue of mass murdering children is just one of the reasons why. You wonder why our country is going down the tubes, you wonder why our land is being polluted with such darkness and immorality? I think it has a lot to do with this sin of mass murdering children, they just want to call it abortion. But don't take my word for it. Let's listen to God's. What happens when a nation and a people, and what happens to the land when people start murdering each other, not just adults but children? This is the account of Cain and Abel. Why are we coming to this? Because it is the first one accountable for the first murder. Let's see how God feels about it and what consequences there are when you are guilty of murder, including the murder of children.

Genesis 4: 1-12: "Adam lay with his wife Eve, and she became pregnant and gave birth to Cain. She said, 'With the help of the Lord I have brought forth a man.' Later she gave birth to his brother Abel. Now, Abel kept flocks, and Cain worked in the soil. In the course of time Cain brought some of the fruits of the soil as an offering to the Lord. But Abel brought fat portions from some of the firstborn of his flock. (That was the best part. Fat is actually where you get the good taste. He's not just bringing a portion; he is bringing the fat portion. He's bringing God the best. And he is bringing veal, the young, fresh meat, not an aged cow from up on the hill, he brought the best. Do you see the difference between the two? One gave leftovers and the other gave the best.) The Lord looked with favor on Abel and his offering, but on Cain and his offering he did not look on with favor. (Why? Because it was leftovers. We don't give him leftovers, do we? Our left-over time, our left-over treasure, our left-over tongue, our left-over talents.) So, Cain was very angry, and his face was downcast. Then the Lord said to Cain, 'Why are you angry? Why is your face downcast? If you do what is right, will you not be accepted? (Give God the best, He's God. He deserves the best.) But if you do not do what is right, sin is crouching at your door; it desires to have you, but you must master it.' Now Cain said to his brother Abel, 'Let's go out to the field.' And while they were in the field, Cain attacked his brother Abel and killed him. (You do realize that God sees everything. He sees every child being murdered. People want to play the game that it's not a baby inside. You can't see it, but God sees it, He sees the child, He's the one that gave that child, at the moment of conception, life, and He is there when the people literally suck that child to pieces or tear it apart.) Then the Lord said to Cain 'Where is your brother Abel?' 'I don't know,' he replied. 'Am I my brother's keeper?' The Lord said, 'What have you done? Listen! Your brother's blood cries out to me from the ground. Now you are under a curse and driven from the ground, which opened its mouth to receive your brother's blood from your hand. When you work the ground, it will no longer yield its crops for you. You will be a restless wanderer on the earth.'"

So, God sees every murder that is going on. It brings a curse upon the people who partake of it, it curses the land and He was cast out. That was the first murder. Now, let's fast forward to another verse dealing with murder. God takes it seriously. Cain was banished, he was cursed for killing his brother.

Numbers 35: 30-33 "Anyone who kills a person is to be put to death as a murderer only on the testimony of witnesses. But no one is to be put to death on the testimony of only one witness. Do not accept a ransom for the life of a murderer, (Bribery doesn't go on today in the courtrooms does it?) who deserves to die. He must surely be put to death. Do not accept a ransom for anyone who has fled to a city of refuge and so allow him to go back and live on his own land before the death of the high priest. Do not pollute the land where you are. (So, what pollutes the land? Blood.) Bloodshed pollutes the land, and atonement cannot be made for the land on which blood has been shed, except by the blood of the one who shed it. Do not defile the land where you live and where I dwell for I the Lord, dwell among the Israelites."

So, what we see is murder, it's obviously something that God does not like. He abhors it. There are stiff penalties when it comes to murdering somebody, be it an adult or a child. Murder is wrong, that is why when you look at the Ten Commandments, what is right there in the middle? Do not murder! That is what is going on there as we see in the scripture. God takes it very seriously. But that is exactly what is going on with abortion. And it's not just murder, it's the mass murder of people. And not just people, but the people who are the most vulnerable, the people who are the most innocent, children. And it's the mass murder of them. So, do you think that it has any affect in polluting our society? Polluting our land? Do you think that is inviting the curse, the judgement of God upon our nation? And upon people who do that? Absolutely! Because God absolutely hates murder. And again, we're not talking about just one or two, a couple instances here or there. We already saw the stats, over 60,000,000 children have been mass murdered through this abortion movement in the US alone and 1.5 billion children have been murdered through abortion around the world, and God sees every one of them.

So, you wonder why the Israelites were exiled from the land? It was still their land, but God exiled them from it, and they were sent into captivity. The land got polluted. The thing is, when you start to take a look at what is going on, not only early in Numbers, but the Israelites were told, do not murder in Exodus, before that. You have the Ten Commandments saying that you shall not murder. God gives stiff penalties for murder and here is what you are supposed to do. If they murder someone, make sure you get your witnesses right, and it is legit, they need to go too. You cannot let this get out of control. But not only did the Israelites not do that, they also violated what God said, when you go into the nations, the land that I give you, do not follow and do the detestable practices of those nations. He said if you don't get rid of them, they are going to be thorns in your eyes and barbs in your side. Basically, they are going to seduce you to do whatever they do. Now, believe it or not, God said repeatedly from the Genesis account, in Exodus with the Ten Commandments, and what we just saw in Numbers, even here in a civil issue, how you are supposed to deal with murders, if it were to unfortunately happen, they not only continue to do so, but they, got involved in child murder. Ours today is called abortion. But all it is, is the mass murder of children. Because we are taking it to a scale that is even beyond what happened with the Israelites. They called it the worship of Molech. Now let me give you a picture of this. This is really what was going on. Basically, you can see that giant idol of Molech and you can see that there is a fire burning underneath and it would heat that statue up from the inside out. They would literally throw children on to Molech. They would do it for personal gain and for personal convenience. Exactly the same thing that is being done today. Now let me give you a couple variances in case you're looking. It was not only called

Molech, it was also called Moloch, also in the scripture it is the same entity, Milcam or Malcam. The word actually meant King or Great King. This is what they thought was their great king and this great king needed to be appeased by murdering children. The scripture talks about this repeatedly. Rabbinical tradition depicted Molech as a bronze statue heated with fire into which the victims were thrown, the babies. In fact, this is not some myth. Archeological excavations since the 1920's have produced evidence for child sacrifices, so there's tons of evidence that this is what was going on. What they did, is when they put the kids into the arms of Molech, as he was heated up super-hot, they called that 'passing through the fire.' That was the practice, the offerings were passing through the fire, and again they were children. This was an act of worship. So-called worship. This is what the nations were doing. God said don't have anything to do with this. Don't follow their detestable practices. Don't do this, and

when you get in there, you had better clean house and clean the land or they are going to suck you in and that's exactly what happened. The Israelites got involved in this. I'm not talking about just the pagan nations around them, the Israelites got involved in the mass murder of children.

First, they would just do one or two at a time, then they would put more and more in there. In fact, every time a child was placed into the molten hot arms of that statue, the priest would spread out their arms too, towards the outstretched hands, and say this, "They are not men but oxen, oxen, oxen," repeatedly. So, they literally treated the babies like they were just a cattle sacrifice. Then they would exclaim to the statue, Molech, "Lord eat!" Eat, children, burn them alive! And then, they would call upon Molech to pour out rain and bring forth. So why were they doing this? Because they got convinced of this so-called statue. A demon, a demon is behind every idol, scripture is clear about that. So, you are dealing with a demonic practice. But they did it because they believe that that thing would give them prosperity. Sound familiar? It's the same thing that's going on today.

The statue got so hot that when the babies were scarcely at the edge of the opening, they disappeared like a drop of water on a red-hot plate and white smoke rose amid the scarlet color, the blood. Children! Nevertheless, the god was not appeased. He wished for even more. In order to appease him, a larger supply of the victims were piled up on his hands by a big chain above them to hold them in place. You can't just give one, it was taking too long so they would chuck more and more kids into the arms of the statue. Imagine the scene. To keep them from falling and going around and being consumed they would chain them in place. They attempted to make amends by sacrificing. They thought they had made Molech mad, so they needed to appease him. So, they made attempts to make amends by sacrificing 200 children of the best families at once. Now how sick is that?

That's not a god, that's a demon. But the real God, He deserves the best. We have a tendency to give Him leftovers. Yet here are these people worshiping an idol, a demon, with this grievous behavior and they are giving him the best. So, you see the twisted irony there? Then they got so excited that they sacrificed above and beyond that, 200 to 300 children all at once. Three hundred children were sacrificed. Oh, and then it also states that the nobles acquired and raised children, not of their own, for the express purpose of sacrificing them to Molech. So not only would they be willing to sacrifice their own children, but hey, if you really want to get prosperous and have all the prosperity poured out upon you, and you can only give birth so often, they literally would get kids of other parents and raise them to be used as sacrifices. This was what really went on there.

Again, the Israelites got involved in this. Another account tells us, with full knowledge and understanding, they offered up their own children. Those who had no children would buy little ones from poor people. Meanwhile, the mother stood by without a tear or a moan. You know why? Here's what was going on. Should she utter a single moan or let a single tear fall, she would forfeit the money they promised to pay for her child and the child would be sacrificed anyway. So, she had to sit there emotionless as her child is burned alive. Or you don't get the what? Money! Sound familiar today? It's the exact horrible procedure. I can't believe it's being repeated today. The whole area before the statue was filled with, what? You might wonder, how can these people stand there while these babies are being chucked into this Molech thing, again and again, repeatedly? How can people stand there and deal with that? Children screaming, vehemently, being burned alive! Have you ever got burned? Imagine being put on a skillet. I hate to be graphic, but this is what was really going on, multiple kids. In the context of what we are dealing with, it is a graphic issue. They should have said stop, stop, but you know what they did? They distracted people.

Because they didn't want them to hear the cries of the children being burned alive, here's what they would do. The whole area before the statue would be filled with a loud noise of flutes and drums so that the cries of the children could not reach the ears of the people. Isn't that interesting? That is what is going on today, call it Planned Parenthood all you want. I call them ministers of Molech. That's really what is going on. It's the exact same thing. It's all about money. And you know why people are not in an uproar? Because the media is distracting everybody from this issue. As you saw before they are doing it with their varying on terminology. When somebody comes up to you, "You mean to tell me you are against abortion?" I answer, "Yes I am. I'm very strongly against anyone murdering a child!" They reply, "You mean to tell me that you think that fetus is a viable child?" I answer, "Yes, I believe that every child at the moment of conception is a real live baby and nobody has the right to do that." They reply, "You mean to tell me that a woman doesn't have the right to choose?" I answer, "No one, man or woman has the right to murder a child!" You see, they are hiding, like with the flutist, when you look over here at what is really going on, people will freak out. And that's the game that is being played. In their very verbiage, so don't fall for that. Number two, the media refuses to show what's going on and in the previous chapter we saw that the church also refuses to show what's going on. So, the only place you are going to get it is from those of us that will stand up and speak on behalf of the innocent ones who are being sacrificed by the millions, by a modern day Molech system called Planned Parenthood. That's what's going on.

They are trying to get us off track of what is really going on. Because they know that if the truth comes out, and people begin to realize what is really happening to these children, the debate is over. Why do you see in the news that they refuse to show what is really happening to these children? If they were to show just one clip for 60 seconds, or even 30 seconds, of what remains after murdering these children, it's over, case closed, it's done. Because any human person that saw a pile of human baby body parts would say that ought not to be done. We've got to stop this right now. That's why they won't do it. Why do you think that is? I think it's because they don't want the truth to get out. You can see why God is totally abhorred about this. In fact, God not only told the Israelites don't you dare murder, period, child or adult, and he gave stiff penalties because he does not like murder. But again, He told the Israelites repeatedly, "Whatever you do, don't you dare get involved in this Molech and child sacrifice." Let me give you some of the scriptures that talk about this and God's very strong about it.

Leviticus 18:21 "Do not give any of your children to be sacrificed to Molech, for you must not profane the name of your God. I am the Lord."

Leviticus 20:2 "Say to the Israelites: 'Any Israelite or any alien living in Israel who gives any of his children to Molech must be put to death. The people of the community are to stone him.'"

Put him to death, you cannot allow that to go on.

Leviticus 20:3 "I will set my face against that man and I will cut him off from his people. For by giving his children to Molech, he has defiled my sanctuary and profaned my holy name."

Does it sound like God's abhorred by this? Stiff penalties for this? This is the same thing that is going on today. Scripture calls it Molech, child sacrifice, today it is called Planned Parenthood. Abortion, it's the exact same thing. That's us.

Leviticus 20:4 "If the people of the community (now this one is for those that know what is going on and refuse to do anything) close their eyes when that man gives one of his children to Molech and they fail to put him to death."

Leviticus 20:5 "I will set my face against that man and his family and will cut off from their people both him and all who follow him in prostituting themselves to Molech."

So now you know what's going on, but you refuse to say anything about it. That's a judgement on people today, dare I say, who refuse to talk about this. How many would say that God takes this seriously? Now here's the good news. King Josiah was one of the good kings, if you remember. Israel had good kings and bad kings, they had the ten northern tribes and the two southern tribes. Most of the northern tribes were bad and the southern tribes had a few good ones, then the bad guys came in and all of them went into exile. But this was a revival time with King Josiah and here is what he did.

2 Kings 23:10 "He (Josiah) desecrated Topheth, (Topheth was one of the places where they were sacrificing children) which was in the Valley of Ben Hinnom, (Or valley of Gehenna) so no one could use it to sacrifice his son or daughter in the fire to Molech."

So, what did King Josiah do? Why did the state of Israel flourish while he was King? Amongst other reforms, he got rid of their ability to mass murder children. What do you think would happen if we as a nation did that today? Could we experience revival?

Jeremiah 32:35 "They built high places for Baal in the Valley of Ben Hinnom to sacrifice their sons and daughters to Molech though I never commanded, nor did it enter my mind, that they should do such a detestable thing and so make Judah sin."

Come on, are you serious? Now you are murdering children! How far can you go? You can kind of feel it in the text of what God is talking about there. This is why God offered up such a stiff punishment. This is why the land gets polluted, this is why they were judged, this is why they went off into exile. There were other sins too, but a lot of it had to do with this stuff. This was a big one and God repeatedly warned them more than once. Not only did He hold accountable those who were doing it, but those who saw it, knew it, and did nothing about it. How many times do we hear stories about the German people who knew what was going on in the concentration camps and did nothing? We will sit there and say, 'Oh, those people, how could they, while they could smell the smoke, they could see the smoke, they could hear the cries, they knew what was going on in those trains, but they didn't speak up, they did nothing.' But we judge them, saying, how sick. But, do we stand up for the innocent children being murdered by the tens of millions? Do we speak up? Oh no, they might get mad at us, my boss might fire me. The same thing is going on today.

But notice it was said that it was taking place in the Valley of Hinnom. The Valley of Hinnom in Hebrew is the Valley of Gehenna. Gehenna was the place that the fires were burning to murder the children with Molech. Jesus used this place to describe Hell. This is a great word study. Gehenna was where they did child sacrifice.

Matthew 5:22 "Whoever shall say, 'You fool,' shall be guilty enough to go into Gehenna."

Gehenna translated into the English is Hell. But what is it? It's the same place where the children were being sacrificed. He likens it unto Hell.

Matthew 5:29 "It is better for you that one of the parts of your body perish, than for your whole body to be thrown into Gehenna."

Matthew 5:30 "Better for you that one of the parts of your body perish, than for your whole body to go into Gehenna."

Matthew 10:28 "Rather fear Him who is able to destroy both soul and body in Gehenna."

Matthew 18:9 "It is better for you to enter life with one eye, than with two eyes to be thrown into Gehenna."

Matthew 23:15 "Woe to you, scribes and Pharisees, hypocrites, because you ... make one proselyte twice as much a child of Gehenna as yourselves."

Matthew 23:33 to the Pharisees "You serpents, you brood of vipers, how shall you to escape the sentence of Gehenna?"

Mark 9:43 "It is better for you to enter life crippled, than having your two hands, to go into Gehenna into the unquenchable fire."

Mark 9:45 "It is better for you to enter life lame, than having your two feet, to be cast into Gehenna."

Mark 9:47 "It is better for you to enter the Kingdom of God with one eye than having two eyes, to be cast into Gehenna."

Luke 12:5 "Fear the One who, after He has killed has authority to cast into Gehenna; yes, I tell you, fear Him."

So here is a hellish practice, murdering children, in the flames of a sick statue, for profit, for personal convenience, for personal gain, and it was happening in this place called Gehenna. And Jesus said, "You want to know what Hell is like? Look at that place." Very graphic. God does not condone this, He abhors it. Serious punishment is going on. This is why God told the Israelites repeatedly, don't you dare, don't you dare, don't be a part of this. But they did it anyway and what happened? See you later. They were exiled. Again, this is what is going on today. You wonder why the wrath of God is coming on our planet for seven years non-stop? You wonder why our nation is polluted with so much darkness and immorality? We haven't seen the end of it, unfortunately.

Here's another way to demonstrate the game that they play. Remember I said that they play the game with the media today, how they use their terminology? It's like, don't let the people see what is going on, like they did with the music and the flutes. Just distract them so they don't see what's really going on. It's another way that they are trying to distract us from acknowledging what this really is. What they do is they say, 'We can't see inside of the womb.' It's just there, somehow, because it's hidden under skin, then that's not a real baby. Again, don't call it a baby because everybody knows what a baby is, we will call it a fetus. And it's not even a real human. It's just a blob of tissue. And here's the latest term they use, it's not a *viable human*. Do you understand what they mean by that? They say it's not human because it's not a viable human. Meaning, if they take that child out of the womb, it can't survive on its own. It's not viable, therefore it's not human. Well, let me strip you of all your clothes and throw you out in the Antarctica and see how long you last. And by the way, when the child gets outside the womb, what do you expect it to do? Go get a job? Drive a car? Go to the store? Shop for its own food? Look at what a ridiculous statement that is. That is the actual argument they make though. It's not really human because it's not viable, because if you take it outside, it will die. It must not be a human. Are you serious? They are playing the flute to distract you from what is really going on!

Now what we are going to deal with in this chapter, that was just the introduction, is that we are going to expose the distraction. That these are real children who are getting brutally murdered, torn apart alive, or sucked apart alive, or put in this saline solution that is meant to kill the child inside and out. We are going to expose that. The best way to do that is from the many, many, people that have survived their own murder attempt. The survivors, because to me, how do you call that a blob of tissue? That's an adult right now who is saying I survived my own murder attempt. Do you see what I'm saying? You can play your music all you want and distract with your terminology, but these people survived their murder attempt. What are you going to say now, that they are not viable? It's not a real child? It's a real person, saying that they were a real child, being murdered. So, I want to share with you some of those survivors.

I want to expose to you the excuse that we don't really know if the child is really a child, because it's inside the womb, that's the game that is played. It's not a real baby. Well you have no excuse, nowadays. First of all, we know it's not true, we know that biblically, life begins at conception. But we also have technology that shows you that, yes, it's hidden inside the womb, under the skin, in the belly, it's a real baby. It's a real baby that you are killing. We have gone from 2D to 3D to what is now called 4D sonograms. Let's take a look at this technology we have that shows that that child, beyond any shadow of a doubt, is a real child. This is a viable human to use their own terminology. This is a real baby.

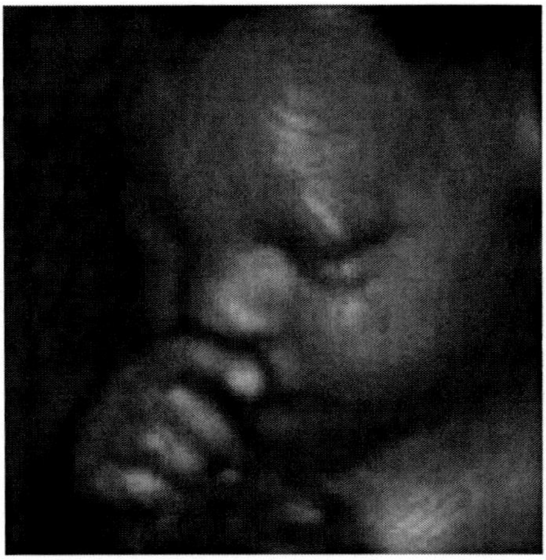

"The standard common obstetric diagnostic mode is 2D scanning. 2D ultrasounds are standard medical protocol for anyone that is pregnant. Ultrasounds allow the medical professional to take a much-needed look at the developing baby. The 2D standard ultrasound relies on sound waves. The sound waves are sent in a straight line until they are reflected back from an object inside the mother to be. It then reflects the amazing image of the growing baby on the screen. Recent technology now allows us to capture an image unlike anything before. With groundbreaking 3D technology, we can now produce a realistic first look at your little wonder. It is one of the biggest things to come along for pregnant families. It has gone on to become the number one way that family's bond with their unborn baby. In 3D imaging the same sound wave technology is used, the only difference is, instead of sound waves being sent straight down and reflected back as in 2D, the sound waves are sent at different angles. The returning echoes are then processed by a sophisticated computer program. Resulting in the reconstructed 3D image of your baby. With this technology you are now able to see more than just that skeletal image. You can actually see whose nose the baby has and who he or she looks like."

There is no excuse but that is their distracting thing, just like Molech, play the flute, play the music, don't let them deal with reality or they are going to freak out and all this will crumble. Oh, I'm sure it's just a blob of tissue, not a viable human. No, that is a real baby. You know it, we all know it. But why don't they show it on the media? Because if you show that on the media, on the news station, it's over. It's instantly over. Because that is a real baby. You should have listened to God the whole time. I shouldn't have to show you the technology. But we have the technology and there really is no excuse but they refuse to air it.

Lets get to those survivors. Here is the first one we are going to take a look at. How do you explain this one? If she wasn't a real child, then she wasn't a baby being torn apart. Now what you would notice about Ana Rosa is that she doesn't have an arm. That is because her arm was ripped off in a failed murder attempt. You may call it abortion but it was a

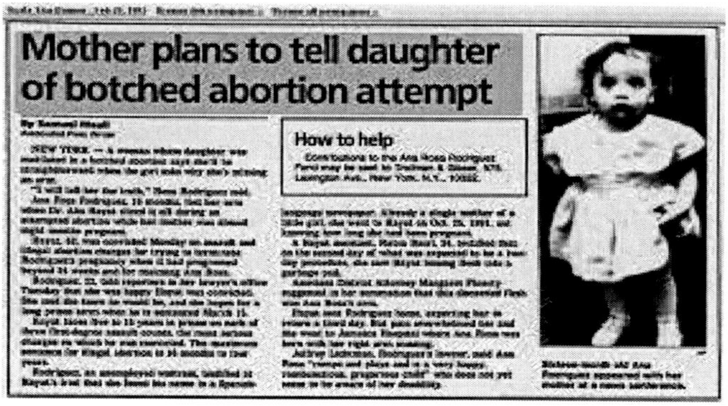

Mother plans to tell daughter of botched abortion attempt

How to help

failed murder attempt. That is why her arm is missing. In fact here are some more gruesome details about her failed murder attempt.

Prolife American reports: *"When we first adopted Sheila, at that same time we heard the story about little Ana Rosa Rodriguez. This scumbag abortionist named Abu Hayat in New York had sold Ana Rosa Rodriguez's mom, he sold her mom and her mom's boyfriend an abortion. He started doing the abortion and he pulls out an arm and he looks at this arm and he says, 'Wait, this baby is further along than I thought. I didn't charge enough money.'*

"Literally, this is what he said. She's on the operating room table. He goes out into the waiting room and confronts the boyfriend and says, I need another $500.00 or $800.00 and the boyfriend says I don't have any money. We gave you all the money we had for the abortion. The doctor says well it's not enough because she is further along than what we thought she was. So he didn't finish the abortion.

"He dismisses her. He's got the arm of this baby in his abortion room. That night she goes into labor and delivers the baby. The baby is 34 or 35 weeks or maybe 37 weeks, somewhere around there, perfectly healthy but missing her right arm. When they told the story at the hospital, the authorities went back to the abortion clinic and found her arm to confirm the story.

"This sleezball abortionist, no that is a redundent statement, they are all sleezballs. I saw that show with Donahue. If I could have reached through that television screen and grabbed him. Let me tell you, he comes on that show and he's holding this little girl, this little child, with her mother on the panel and I'll never forget this as long as I live.

"He says look at this beautiful child of God and says, 'Now we have a very emotional show today, but I want you people to understand that this does not make a statement about the right to choose.' And I'm thinking that if it doesn't make a statement about the right to choose, what does it make a statement about? The little girl has an arm that was pulled off by a sleazebag abortinist and this doesn't make a statement to you, about the right to choose?

"We had just got Sheila and I'm looking at Sheila and looking at the picture from the ad, and I still have the picture, of Ana Rosa Rodriguez, with a big bandage wrapped around her top because she has no arm. I tell you, it just overwhelmed

me with sadness and then unbelievable anger towards these people. I know that's not right to have those kinds of feelings and I know that God probably doesn't approve of that sort of sentiment, but I can't help it."

Interviewer: "*I think you might be right, but God says in your anger do not sin. He's giving us permission for the anger. That righteous indignation and comtempt that we have for the abortion industry, I think is God's feeling toward abortion."*

Must be reading the Bible because God absolutely abhors it. Did you catch that part where he was talking about Donahue? Do you remember that show? He was talking about when Donahue brought on Ana Rosa Rodriguez, held her up to the audience with her missing arm and said look at this beautiful child of God, and then proceeded to make the disclaimer that this has nothing to do with a woman's right to choose. What do you do with that? You're holding the evidence in your arms of one who is missing an arm from an attempted murder. Now believe it or not, that doctor, and this is from the New York Times, 1993, in New York, oh how times have changed, he was actually convicted of this. Here is the article.

New York Times: *"An east coast doctor was convicted yesterday for performing an illegal 3rd trimester abortion,* (i.e. a murder attempt on a baby), *when he severed the arm of the baby. Dr. Abu Hayat was guilty of assault on Rosa Rodrigues and her baby Ana Rosa. The prosecution argued that Dr. Hayat had cared more about money than his patients. The 64-year-old doctor faces a maximum sentence of twenty and one third years to sixty-one years, the equivalent of a life sentence."*

And what is New York doing now? You can kill them all the way up to birth. Remember the way they were applauding it? Oh, how times have changed.

New York Times: *"Dr. Hayat was also convicted of two counts from another patient, a lady by the name of Marie Moise on whom he performed an incomplete abortion. Mrs. Moise's husband David testified that the doctor had said that the price would be $300.00 and stopped midway through the procedure and demanded an additional $500.00.*

Mr. Moise testified that when he insisted that he could not produce the money that the doctor forced him to leave the office with his bleeding, semi-conscience, wife and the next day Mrs. Moise began a weeklong stay at St. Luke's Hospital for treatment of a severe infection that the doctors said was caused by pieces of the dismembered baby left in her uterus.

The authorities have described Dr. Hayat's office at 9th Avenue A, as an abortion mill. More than forty women came forward to say that Dr. Hayat botched their abortions and officials said that his error during one abortion killed a patient, a 17-year-old girl, but no charges were brought against him for that."

Oh, we haven't even got to the aftermath of abortion. That will be in the next chapter. Women's lives that are utterly destroyed when they get duped to go along with this and believe this is just a blob of tissue. But that was just the first survivor that we are dealing with. There are multiple ones. But this is to unmask their distracting, diversionary tactic. What's going on here, play the music, turn it up, put your head in the sand, it's not a real baby. How do you explain these people coming out alive? Now that was a baby girl. We didn't get to hear from her, so let's hear from people directly who survived their own murder attempt.

The first one we are going to deal with is Gianna Jessen. She is very active in pro-life, obviously, having been there and done that. But let's see what happened to her, how do you explain this one, was she just a blob of tissue? Was she not a viable human? What is she doing walking around today telling people what went on?

.

Mike Huckabee: *"My next guest knows all too well the loss of human potential due to abortions. That's because she was intended to be a victim of an abortion. She was born during a botched abortion, which is the only medical procedure that is considered a failure when the patient lives. It left her with cerebral palsy, and she was branded by doctors as a hopeless case who would never even lift her head. Boy, did she prove them wrong. She's a marathon runner, a sought-after speaker, a singer, and a voice for the truly voiceless. I'm so honored to welcome to the show, Gianna Jessen. Gianna it is an honor and a thrill to have you here."*

Gianna Jessen: "*I'm so excited to meet you.*"

Mike Huckabee: "*Thank you. Your story is just incredible. Let's start when you first knew about the circumstances of your birth.*"

Gianna Jessen: "*Well, my life has always been unconventional. I'm adopted, and I learned of the circumstances on Christmas Day at 12 years old.*"

Mike Huckabee: "*What a Christmas present.*"

Gianna Jessen: "*It was interesting.*"

Mike Huckabee: *How did your adoptive parents break the news to you and what did they say?*"

Gianna Jessen: "*Well, I was always asking my mother why I have cerebral palsy and she would say because you were a premature baby or because you had a traumatic birth, and both were true. But I was never satisfied with those answers. I was always asking over and over again, and on that day, she said do you really want to know? I said yep and she let me know. And I said, for a 12-year-old, well at least I have cerebral palsy for a good reason.*"

Mike Huckabee: "*What did happen at your birth. You found this out at 12 and obviously you have been very open and honest about it but explain what took place when your birth mother attempted to have you aborted.*"

Gianna Jessen: "*I would be happy to explain that but one thing that is really, really, bothering me, if I may, and that is, I know that right now there are people watching that are flipping out. They have stuffed down abortion for 25 years and how dare they say she went through this, how dare she say that, and I just want to say, peace to you, because I am a believer in Jesus and if you will just give Him those abortions and you ask Him to forgive you and set you free, He will.*

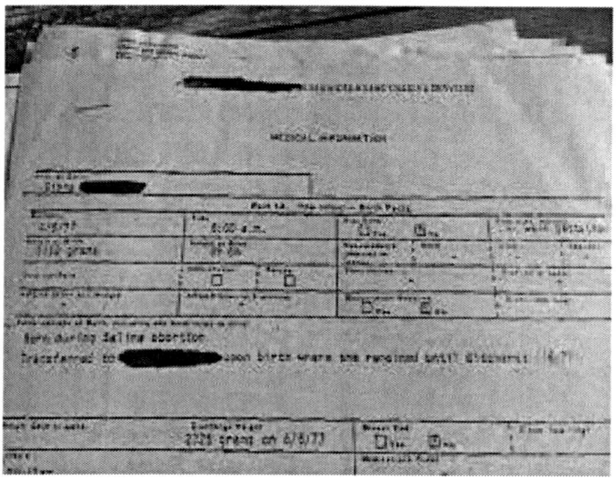
[redacted]
MEDICAL INFORMATION
Born during Saline abortion
Transferred to [redacted] upon birth where she remained until discharge
2325 grams on 6/6/77

So anyway, my biological parents were 17, my biological mother was 7 ½ months pregnant and she went to Planned Parenthood. They said that she was too young to have a baby, you need to go have a late term saline abortion. A saline abortion is a saline/salt solution that is injected into the mother's womb. The baby gulps that solution, it is to burn the baby inside and out, blinds and suffocates the child and then the baby will be born dead within 24 hours.

Except to everyone's great shock and surprise, instead of being born dead I was born alive, 6:00 in the morning, April 6, 1977. It says on the medical records 'born during Saline abortion, transferred to upon birth... where she remained until discharge, 29 ½ weeks, 2 ½ lbs.' It is common practice for abortionists to strangle a baby that survives, suffocate the baby or leave the baby there to die.

But the only reason I am sitting right here is because of Jesus Christ and also because He delayed the abortionist. It was only 6:00 in the morning, he wasn't even at work yet. Had he been there he would have ended my life. But a nurse called an ambulance and got me transferred to a hospital, thereby saving my life. They said this kid's not going to make it, this kid's going to die, well, I didn't die. But after not dying I was placed in an emergency foster care with a bunch of morons who decided they didn't like me so they would shut me in a room for a long period of time.

I was taken out of that home and placed into another home, a beautiful woman's home by the name of Penny. By this time, I was 17 months old, 32 lbs. of dead weight and was diagnosed with cerebral palsy, which is caused directly by the lack of oxygen to my brain while I was surviving an abortion. So, you can imagine how I feel when I hear the argument that if the baby is disabled, we need to terminate the pregnancy. Well, who are you, healthy person, to look at me and decide for me what my quality of life is? You have no idea how beautiful my life is because I have something I have to overcome. Because I actually need Jesus!

Mike Huckabee: "*So many people...*"

Gianna Jessen: "*Those people are on crack!*"

Mike Huckabee: "*Yes they are, to be blunt.*"

All right, how do you deny that? How do you explain that one away? How can you sit there and still say that that is not a viable human in there? That it's just a blob of tissue. She survived her own murder attempt. In fact, she is very active today, just to give you a little background. Obviously, she is a huge pro-life advocate, and also a disability rights advocate, because once again, one of the other justifications isn't that you just don't want the child, but now they are being proactive to get you to go ahead and kill your child because there might be a chance that it could be disabled and who wants one of those kids? She also campaigned against abortion saying, *"It's more comfortable for people to think of abortion as a political decision or a right, but I am not a right, I am a human being."* She has done all kinds of activist stuff here in the United States and around the world. In 2002 she was there at the signing of the Born Alive Innocence Protection Act, then under President George W. Bush, she was in London to support helping the reduction of the number of abortions under the UK Abortion Act. She's been there at the Parliamentary meeting and House of Commons, she was at the Colorado State House of Representatives, she was in Australia to lobby Federal politicians on late term abortions. The same month, in 2008, she appeared in a political advertisement during the 2008 U.S. Presidential campaign and she said this, *"If Barack Obama had his way, I wouldn't be here."* Because he wanted no restrictions on the murdering of children, and of course, he opposed the Born Alive Legislation.

Recently she was a part of the Congressional Hearings investigating Planned Parenthood, after the body parts were being sold and caused a bit of a ruckus there. During her testimony she asked Planned Parenthood the following question, *"If abortion is about women's rights, then where were mine?"* She's a woman. If it's all about women's rights, how come she didn't get any? How come she had to try to survive her own murder attempt? Wow, interesting! So how do you deny this? You can't ignore the technology, because you can see it's a baby, these people are surviving. How do you explain that and how can you act like it's not real, how can you sit there and try to justify it?

But let me give you another one. The next murder survivor is Melissa Ohden. She too survived her attempted murder with saline solution. Let's take a look at her account.

Melissa Ohden: *"I have known ever since I can remember that I had not only been adopted but that I had been born about 4 months premature and I knew that I had been very sick and that I was very tiny and the doctors didn't have a very good prognosis for my life. To me, I didn't have a lot of questions about growing up, I guess, it didn't matter because I was healthy, I was in a great home, I was loved, and life was good."*

CBN reports: *"But Melissa only knew part of the story. She was 14 when her older sister got pregnant out of wedlock and considered an abortion. Melissa's* *mother wanted to stop her daughter from having the abortion and told her daughter the shocking circumstances of Melissa's birth."*

Melissa Ohden: *"She said, no, we never meant to keep it from you. There was no easy way to tell you this. Please know that we will always love you. And then she just kind of blurted it out. No, Melissa, your mother had an abortion during her 5th month of pregnancy with you and you survived it."*

CBN Reports: *"In 1978 Melissa's 17-year-old birth mother walked into an abortion clinic expecting to walk out with her problem solved. She chose a saline injection to end the life of her 5-month-old baby. When the procedure was over a nurse heard her 2 lb. baby crying from the discarded medical waste. Social Services knew Mr. & Mrs. Cross wanted to adopt another baby girl, but they didn't know if they would take such a high-risk baby.*

Linda Cross: *When we first saw Melissa, her head was shaved from temple to temple and because she was too little to suck and they fed her intravenously. They told us all the things that could be wrong with her because of the premature birth. As soon as they put her in my arms, I knew she was going to be fine. She was just beautiful. Absolutely beautiful.*

CBN Reports: *Melissa recovered completely and lived a normal childhood until the circumstances of her birth were revealed. Now questions flooded her mind."*

Melissa Ohden: *"The biggest question was, why? Why could you make that decision to end my life? Could I have been so unwanted and so unloved by them, even though I knew Jesus loved me, my family loved me, but it could not take away the pain."*

CBN Reports: *"Melissa is now married and there is no doubt in her mind that God saved her for a purpose. And part of that purpose is, she says, sharing her story of life with the world and she treasures being a mother herself.*

Melissa Ohden: *"I know that was the Lord's plan for me also because all those years I just desperately wanted to be a mother. I was very scared. I had to heal from a lot of pain about my life, so I didn't want to become a mother until I felt like I was whole."*

CBN reports: *"Ironically, Melissa gave birth to Olivia in the same hospital that her own life was supposed to end.*

Melissa Ohden*: "I literally used to drive past that hospital gripping the wheel of my car because it was so hurtful for me to know that was the building that I struggled for my life. Now I can drive past that hospital with my head held high because it holds the most beautiful memories that I will ever hold in life. There is no greater gift that a woman can give, than the life of a child, and if she believes that she can't provide for that child forever, then the next best thing she can do for that child is to give them the joy of being with another family for adoption."*

Can I translate that? There is no excuse ever to murder a child. Even in the case of rape. If you don't want to have the child, why is it that the child has to be the one to be punished? Not just punished, murdered, for something it had nothing to do with. Put the baby up for adoption. The child does not have to die.

Melissa Ohden is very active in pro-life circles. She is a pro-life public speaker, has testified before Congress against Planned Parenthood and about the baby parts. She also criticized Barack Obama's voting record on legislation to protect infants born alive during abortions because he was wanting it to continue. She has been on various TV and Radio programs, Family Radio, 700 Club, Fox News, The Mike Huckabee show, her life story is told in *A Voice for Life*, a pro-life documentary, she has two non-profit organizations called *The Abortion Survivors Network* and another one called *For Olivia's Sake*, which is her daughter. The latter is intended to raise awareness of the ripple effect abortion has on men, women, children, families and communities, as again, it destroys anyone that gets involved with it. She has said, *"Parents of an unborn child often fail to consider how their decisions affect others. My daughter would never have had life if my murder attempt had succeeded. My husband would never have a wife if my murder attempt had succeeded. And my adoptive parents would never have had a child if my murder attempt had succeeded."*

At this point, it's pretty much a slam dunk. I mean there is no excuse. I don't need any technology; I don't need these stories. I need to honor the Word of God where God says that he abhors this and scripture is very clear, life begins at conception. You can say you can't see something under that skin, but God says it's a baby, don't even go down that route, don't follow Molech.

But now that we do have the technology and now you hear from people who have survived the murder attempt, it's a slam dunk. Who would continue with this? Well, believe it or not, it is continuing. It's not only continuing, but just like the people who sacrificed the children to Molech, where were those children, inside of the womb, or outside of the womb? We're not just talking about murdering children for profit or gain, we're talking about murdering children outside the womb. That is now what our nation is discussing. For those of you who have forgot, I'm going to remind you. If you recall what started this, and states are jumping on the bandwagon, believe it or not, to now have a discussion on killing a child, after it has been born. All killing of children is wrong but we are now at a stage where we are having a discussion as to whether or not to kill that baby after it's been born. Now that was the fervor that was caused by Virginia Governor Ralph Northam. I'm going to share with you something that is very deceptive. He was responding to another Virginia representative, a doctor, that would explain what the procedure would do, the bill going through that state, and he actually supported it. Here is the discussion that began the great fervor, killing children outside of the womb.

Gilbert: "*How late in the third trimester can a physician perform an abortion if he indicated it would impair the mental health of the woman?*"

Tran: "*Or physical health.*"

Gilbert: *Okay.*"

Tran: "*Okay.*"

Gilbert: "*I'm talking about the mental health.*"

Tran: "*So, I mean, through the third trimester. The third trimester goes all the way to 40 weeks.*"

Gilbert: "*To the end of the third trimester?*"

Tran: *Yup, I don't think we have a limit in the bill.*"

Gilbert: "*Where it's obvious that a woman is about to give birth, that she has physical signs that she is about to give birth. Would that be a time where she could request an abortion, if she was so certified? She's dilating.*"

Tran: "*Mr. Chairman that would be a decision that the doctor, the physician, and the woman would make at that point.*"

Gilbert: "*I understand that. I'm asking if your bill allows that.*"

Tran: "*My bill would allow that. Yes.*"

WTOP Reports: *"It was a very contentious hearing here yesterday when Fairfax County delegate Kathy Tran made her case for lifting restrictions of third trimester abortions as well as other restrictions now in place and she was pressed by a Republican delegate about whether her bill would permit an abortion even when the woman is essentially dilating getting ready to give birth, and she answered that it would permit an abortion at that stage of labor. Do you support her measure, and can you explain her answer?"*

Ralph Northam: *"You know I wasn't there, Julie, and I certainly can't speak for Delegate Tran, but the first thing I would say is this is why decisions such as this should be made by providers or physicians and the mothers and fathers that are involved. So that in this particular example if a mother is in labor. I can tell you exactly what would happen. The infant would be delivered, the infant would be kept comfortable, the infant would be resuscitated if that is what the mother and the family desired, and then a discussion would ensue between the physician and the mother."*

What's the discussion? Whether they can kill that child after it is completely born outside the womb. That is sick, that is infanticide. Now it's still infanticide inside the womb, it's infanticide the whole way through. But our country is now at the point where they are talking about killing children outside the womb, exactly like Molech worship. And we need to speak up. Now when this first started to air, people started to go nuts because this is on tape and he said what he said. "Yep, they're going to have a discussion, that it is their right, to decide to kill this child outside the womb, fully born." But, did you pick up on what they did? They did a diversionary tactic, just like with Molech. You can't have people deal with it, you have to play some music, drown out the noise, look over here because if they see what is going on, they will stop worshiping Molech.

The same thing happened when this thing came out and it created a fervor. It started to create a national fervor. But within a couple of days, you know what the media came out with? They stopped playing the tape on him saying it's okay to murder children outside the womb and they switched to the black face controversary. That's all the media played. Still to this day, do you think that's by chance? It was within a couple of days of that video getting out of the same guy making the statement of murdering children outside the womb. It was done on purpose, I have no problem with saying that, it was not by chance, it was just like with Molech. Distract them! And they are asking him to get out of office because he had his face painted black, not because he promoted murdering children outside the womb. But nobody is talking about it anymore are they? Because it created a fervor and it spiraled out of control, but they snuck that in there. Pretty slick isn't it. It's not just slick, it's evil. You know what it did do, it fired up our President. And you need to support our President because behind the scenes he's speaking up for these children.

Catherine Hadro, Host, EWTN Pro-Life Weekly: "*This is Catherine Hadro coming to you at the top of the show from the White House, where President Donald Trump today met with an abortion attempt survivor and other pro-lifers who had beat the odds just by being born. This meeting comes in the wake of extreme abortion legislation and recent comments from Virginia governor Ralph Northam which sounded like the defense of infanticide.*

President Trump sat down with pro-lifers who our viewers may recognize from the show including Mike Pickering, a young boy who was born at just 20 weeks, Katherine Alexander, a little girl who was adopted after being born with an opiate addiction and abortion attempt survivor Melissa Odhen, who we spoke with right after the meeting. So, tell us about being at the meeting with President Trump. What was it like? What did you get to say to him?"

Melissa Odhen: *"It was absolutely surreal. You have one of those moments when you are going, 'I was meant to be here today, this is what I was called to* *do.' So, sitting in that Oval Office with him and hearing him talk so passionately about his commitment to life and what he is willing to keep doing legislatively to protect lives like mine, it's absolutely surreal. I am just so thankful for him and this administration and the bold moves he continues to make so that lives like mine can be protected in our society."*

Catherine Hadro*: "What is your impression of what President Trump thinks on this extreme abortion legislation that we are continuing to see across the nation?"*

Melissa Odhen: *"You can tell he thinks it is just an abomination. He talked about Governor Northam and his comment in Virginia and about some of the other states making the same aggressive moves against life and I really appreciate how he has made it a battle cry, and this is a movement. He keeps calling it a movement. I love that so much.*

"He said, 'I think there has been more that has been happening in terms of the movement in the last couple weeks than we have seen in a long time and it's because people see what is happening and they are not willing to sit by quietly and remain silent.' He was such a great encouragement for all of us to be moving in our communities to stand up in defense of life."

Wow, what a switch from the previous administration. Did anyone pick up on the play on words there? I did. I'll tell them to you. President Trump, our current President, he considers this child murder an abomination and yet when Obama was the head of the nation, talk about an abomination, he supported it. What a flip. A turnaround of events. Wow is right! Just when you thought it was never going to turn around, that we were losing our voice in support of children, there's some good things going on. And we need to speak up! Capitalize on this momentum, and we need to get the word out. Speak up for not only number one, the innocent children that are getting murdered, still as we sit here, but two, for our own country. There are certain laws being passed in certain states that are starting to restrict this, and I wish there were full restrictions, but at least it's a start. Believe it or not, I just came across an article that said the pro-abortionists, let me rephrase that, the pro-murderers of children, are starting to get alarmed because they are seeing that things are starting to swing to our end of the court. Which really means God is in our court. And you know what that person said? It almost made me sick. You know what their big concern was? That if Roe vs Wade gets overturned, then she would have to live in a country where there would be forced childbirth. Forced childbirth. How horrible that is. My thing is, if you don't like that, then stay out of the bedroom. But we need to speak up because these people aren't going down easy. Even at this stage we still have Planned Parenthood people saying that literally pulling babies apart inside the womb is a humane procedure.

Mr. Goodlatte: "*Ms. Smith, in the precursor to the Gonzales case, the case of Steinburg vs Carhart, Justice Kennedy dissented from the decision to strike down the partial birth abortion ban that was later upheld in the Gonzales case, which was a different ban version. He described at length the testimony provided by abortionist Leroy Carhart about the alternative D&E procedure. The fetus can be alive at the beginning of the dismemberment process and can survive for a time while its limbs are being torn off.*

"Dr. Carhart agreed that when you pull out a piece of the fetus, let's say an arm or a leg and remove that, and at the time of removal of that portion of the fetus, the fetus is alive. Dr. Carhart has observed fetal heartbeat via ultrasound as extensive parts of the fetus are removed and testified that the mere dismemberment of a limb does not always cause death because he knows of a physician who removed an arm of a fetus and to have the fetus go on to be born as a living child with only one arm.

"The conclusion of a D&E abortion, no intact fetus remains and Dr. Carhart's words are 'the abortionist is left with a tray full of pieces.' Justice Kennedy said 'the fetus in many cases dies just as a human adult or child would. It bleeds to death as it is torn from limb to limb.' Ms. Smith do you believe that this practice represents a humane way to die?"

Ms. Smith: "*Let me separate something that I think is getting confused here in this hearing, again and again. Which is a procedure performed on pre-viable fetuses and procedures that are performed on viable fetuses. Both of the women here on this panel are here today because they were viable at the time that the procedures were performed. What you're talking about is pre-viability procedures performed on a fetus that cannot survive outside the womb."*

Mr. Goodlatte: "*Maybe not, Justice Kennedy was talking about a child that was born alive with only one arm because the other had been pulled off already during the abortion procedure. My question to you, if you are going to answer it, is this a humane way to die?"*

Ms. Smith: "*I believe for a fetus, a pre-viable fetus, yes, a D&E procedure is a very humane procedure and it protects the woman and her health and safety more than any other procedure. In fact, it was substituted for....*"

Mr. Goodlatte: "*I going to reclaim my time and just say that your view of humanity and mine are different. I will ask Ms. Jessen and Ms. Odhen very quickly if you support the 'Pain Capable Abortion Act' that has passed in the House of Representatives as awaiting action in the United States Senate.*"

Ms. Jessen: "*I am speechless with Ms. Smith's reply that she thinks that is a humane way to die! I support it!*"

Mr. Goodlatte: "*Ms. Ohden?*"

Ms. Ohden: "*Yes, I do support the 'Pain Capable Abortion Act' and I want to make it clear that I want abortion to be made unthinkable in our country. I want us not to even have a conversation about another act.*"

Mr. Goodlatte: "*Thank you, I agree.*"

And so does God! Your blindness, and the darkened heart, while actually sitting there with two people who survived a murder attempt, and you still say that it's a humane way to die. And you wonder why the wrath of God is coming for seven years nonstop. We need to be like Josiah. We need to not just deal with it, we need to speak up and to stop this now if revival is ever going to come. How many times do we say God Bless America? But if this doesn't stop, God's going to judge America, just like he did the Israelites, for worshiping modern day Molech, Planned Parenthood.

Chapter Five

The Aftermath of Abortion

Now we are going to deal with the aftermath of abortion. We are going to take a look at the testimonies, specifically of women who murdered their children and the damage it has done to them. Because the reality is, all the people suffer and certainly the child. If they do survive, then they are typically left with health problems or the loss of a limb or they die. But the women's rights movement, the feminists and the abortion industry, are convincing them that this is good for you. This is your right. This is your way to express yourself. This will help you; this will benefit your life. All it does, 100% of the time, is destroy women's lives. It's the aftermath of abortion. The reason why is that the Bible is consistent. Abortion, i.e. murdering children, is called a sin. And what does the Bible say about sin? Sin destroys! Including the sin of abortion. You're not going to be blessed by it. You will be destroyed by it. And that is the theme of this chapter. But there is also a law in scripture, and it says, 'you reap what you sow.'

Galatians 6:7-8: "Do not be deceived; God cannot be mocked. A man reaps what he sows. (So, if I plant a corn seed, what am I going to get? You don't get a whale. No, that is what evolution teaches, which is a lie. You're going to get some corn. If you plant some peas what are you going to get? Peas. When you plant something, you're going to get it right back. That is what God is saying, what you sow is what you are going to get. So, here are your two options) The one who sows to please his sinful nature (that's that sinful, rebellious nature, I want it my way or the highway, me, myself, and I, the unholy trinity) from that nature will reap (from that nature you are going to reap a wonderful life, a fulfilling life, you will have freedom beyond your wildest dreams, isn't that what the lie of abortion says? No, you're going to reap destruction) destruction; (But here's your other option) the one who sows to please the Spirit, i.e. God, from the Spirit, will reap eternal life."

So that is the law God put before us, every day, with every single decision. If you want to follow that selfish, sinful nature, and do your own thing, what do you think you are going to get? Destruction. How many times? Half the time? 60% of the time? No, it's 100% of the time. It's like putting corn in the ground, you are going to get corn every time. It's the same thing. If that is your modus operandi, what you do in life, it's all about me, you are going to reap destruction every single time. It's called sin. You have heard me say before. Sin hurts, sin harms, sin destroys and the most loving thing you can do, as Paul tells you in Galatians, 'you who are spiritual, restore a brother who has fallen in sin.' In other words, if you want to demonstrate your spirituality, when you see a brother or sister going down a sinful route, what do you do? Speak up! Why? Sin hurts, sin harms, sin destroys. The last thing you want to do is keep your mouth shut. Right? And how many people are afraid to speak up? Even discipline in the church. Nobody wants to confront issues. But demonstrate your spirituality by loving that person enough to speak up because you see that they aren't ready at this point to admit that they are going down that sinful route and it's going to lead to destruction. I love you enough to speak up and say come back to God's word. It says turn from that path of destruction, come back and do it God's way and be blessed. Isn't that the kind of friends you want? It's the same thing when you are confronting the issue of abortion. You have to speak up because it's going to lead 100% of the time to destruction. And again, not just with the child, we are now going to see it with the ladies.

Children are destroyed through abortion. Women are destroyed, families are destroyed, marriages are destroyed, society itself is destroyed. That's what we saw before with Molech. The land was cursed. The Israelites that followed Molech, sacrificing the babies. It's the same thing today with modern day abortion. They are Molech supporters. Molech worshipers. It destroys the land. So, my question is, why and how do people get tricked into knowingly going down this sinful route of behavior of abortion, murdering of children, and actually think they are going to come out on top, when God says it's a sin? Just like any sin, you are going to be destroyed. How do they get into that trap? Well, it's the same trick, believe it or not, that satan used. The trick he is using on women today is the exact same trick that he used on the very first woman back in the garden. How did satan deceive the first woman? How did man fall? How did satan dupe mankind? Starting with Eve, of course.

Genesis 3:1-7: Now he, the serpent was craftier than any of the wild animals the Lord God had made. He said to the woman, "Did God really say, 'You must not eat from any tree in the garden'?" (stop right there, what was that? Doubt. Is it the same for you today? Do you really think that's a child in there? I don't know about that. You really think that's a baby in there? That is the first step. Doubt.) The woman said to the serpent, "We may eat fruit from the trees in the garden, but God did say, 'You must not eat fruit from the tree that is in the middle of the garden and you must not touch it, or you will die.'" (Death is going to come as a result of this decision. And then what does satan do, he starts with doubt and then,) "You will not surely die," the serpent said to the woman. (It's called a lie. It's the same thing. The same procedure. He did it with the first woman and he is doing it with women today.) "For God knows that when you eat of it your eyes will be opened and you will be like God, knowing good and evil." When the woman saw that the fruit of the tree was good for food (now remember it's all about what I want, not what God wants, you see how she got swayed? Doubt, then lie, and now it's all about me.) and pleasing to the eye, and also desirable for gaining wisdom, she took some and ate it. She also gave some to her husband, who was with her, and he ate it. Then the eyes of both of them were opened, and they realized they were naked; so, they sewed fig leaves together and made coverings for themselves.

This is why Jesus said satan is not only the father of lies but there is a second characteristic he brings out. He calls him a murderer. He says he has been one since the beginning. And what do you think he is talking about? The beginning of creation. It's the same thing.

John 8:42-44 Jesus said to them, If God were your Father, you would love me, for I came from God and now am here. I have not come on my own; but he sent me. Why is my language not clear to you? Because you are unable to hear what I say. You belong to your father, the devil, and you want to carry out your father's desire. He was a murderer from the beginning, not holding to the truth, for there is no truth in him. When he lies, he speaks his native language, for he is a liar and the father of lies.

Which includes the lie of abortion, that it's acceptable, that it's not a baby and you are going to come out on top. It's a lie. Satan is the one that is inspiring this lie of murdering children. Satan is the one that is deceiving ladies into murdering their children, using the same tactic he used back then. Same thing. You've got to understand. I've said this before. I remember an instructor drilled this into my head. It wasn't just that satan lied, he got Eve to doubt, and then lied to mess up their walk with God. He knew that when they sinned, they would die. Do you get it? Satan did it to kill them. That's why Jesus said he is not only a liar and the father of lies but he's a murderer. It was in the beginning and it's the same thing today. Again, ladies think they are going to come out on top, it's not really a baby, and they get tricked into destroying and killing their babies. That's what satan wants and sometimes they even end up killing themselves as we are going to see in this chapter. They can't take it; they know what they did was wrong. This is all coming from satan. If you think that's too harsh, that satan is the one who is inspiring the abortion movement, the mass murder of children, I've got this video. It's very disturbing, but this is a guy who is witnessing outside of an abortion clinic, i.e. a mass murder of children clinic. Remember to use the right terminology. The abortion doctor, the one that has been killing the babies all day long comes out to take a break. If you could only listen to his voice, with his attitude and what he says about murdering children. This is wild. You tell me this is not satanic.

Man with the cell phone: "*Sir, you need to repent sir.*" He is telling the doctor dressed in blue as he comes out of the building. "*You need to repent sir, for murdering babies.*" The doctor is walking towards the cell phone. The doctor walks right up into the man's face.

Doctor: "*Why?*"

Man with the cell phone: "*Because it is a sin before God, sir.*"

Doctor: "*Why, why?*" He breathes out a loud guttural breath. "*Stinky breath!*" As he keeps making this breathing sound into the man's face.

Man with the cell phone: "*Yes it is, it is pretty evil of you sir. I hope and pray that you..., that's what you do to babies, huh?*"

Doctor: "*I love it!*"

Man with the cell phone*: "You love it?"*

Doctor: *"Yeah, I do!"* As he keeps making the guttural sounds in the man's face.

Man with the cell phone: *"I hope you can come to Christ, sir."*

Doctor: "*I will never go to Christ!"*

Man with the cell phone: "*Yes, I hope you can come to Christ."*

Doctor: "*No, I will never go to Christ. I don't listen to Christ!"*

Man with the cell phone: "*You have a darkened heart, sir."*

Doctor: "*I do, I do, very much so."*

Man with the cell phone: "*You will stand in judgement."*

Doctor: "*Yes, I will! Every day.*

Man with the cell phone. "*You will stand before God in judgement."*

Doctor: "*Yes I will, every day."*

Man with the cell phone: "*For the killing of babies..."*

Doctor: *"I love it, I love it!"* More guttural sounds coming from his mouth.

Man with the cell phone: "*You will keep tearing the babies apart."*

Doctor: "*Yes I will! Yes, I will!"* At that point the security guard steps up to the doctor and asks him to go back into the clinic.

That is not natural! It shows you the spirit behind it. There is something satanic going on and I'll tell you why. Who's the liar, who's the father of all lies? Who's the murderer and has been one since the beginning? What's abortion all about? It's about murdering children. Lying to ladies. It's all satanic. This is what's going on. How sick and twisted it has become that our country puts these kinds of laws forth. You would think that they would outlaw this, the mass murder of children, but instead here are the laws we get passed.

If you kill a pre-born sea turtle you get a $100,000 fine and 1 year in prison.

If you kill a pre-born bald eagle you get a $250,000 fine and 2 years in prison.

If you kill a pre-born human being, you get no penalty.

That's your right. Your life is going to be great. And you wonder why the wrath of God is coming upon our nation. But this is what satan does. Our whole nation is being duped. This is what he has been doing since the beginning. He gets people to doubt God's word, that this is a baby, he lies saying it's a blob, and he deceives them into murdering their own child. And sometimes themselves because he is a murderer and has been one since the beginning. It's the same pattern. To further reiterate this lying deception and murderous, satanic behavior that people are falling for, we are going to see several testimonies of ladies that have been there and done that. Let's walk through the process of doubt and deception and deceit that they have gone through.

Now the first lie that satan throws out at these women to get them to murder their children is hey, it's just a blob of tissue. It's just a blob. And since it's just a blob, it's okay to kill the baby. What you are about to read is these people know that it is a baby and they purposely don't let the ladies see it on the ultrasound monitor.

A nurse is walking their next patient down the hall to the room to have the next abortion. These are their testimonies:

"As the nurse was performing the ultrasound, I watched her and she was looking at my baby on the monitor and I asked her, 'Can I see my baby?' She took the monitor, literally with both her hands and turned it away from me."

"As I was watching the monitor, the nurse and the doctor asked me not to watch. They turned the monitor away.

"And I turned to look at the screen and thought that looks like a baby. She got very upset and started yelling, 'Turn around, don't you dare look at that!'"

"We put her on that table, we find just a blob in her abdomen, we all have blobs, men and women have blobs in their abdomens."

"So, at eighteen, just out of high school, I decided to go through with this abortion. I was told it was a blob of tissue."

"I believed it was just a blob of tissue inside my uterus. I did not believe that it was a baby inside at that time."

"They explained it to me, that it was a blob. That it wasn't anything yet."

"But I needed to have this abortion as soon as possible before this blob of tissue turned into a baby."

"The nurse asked me if I was okay with the procedure and I said no I really wasn't because it seemed like it was killing a baby. But they all looked very professional. They showed me a film strip of just blobs of tissue. So, I thought they are the adults, they are the professionals, it must be okay. So, I went ahead with the procedure."

"She told me that it wasn't even a baby yet. That it was just a clump of cells. I didn't know anything about fetal development, so I believed her. In fact, I felt relieved, because I thought if it's not a baby yet, then I'm not doing anything wrong."

"They had the screen turned away from me and I asked to see it and she said. 'I don't think it's a good idea.' I told her no, I really wanted to see it before I went through with it, so she ran the probe across my stomach and turned the screen towards me and showed me a dot on the screen. I thought, that's it. Well I can do this. I bought the lie. I now know that she didn't show me my baby. She just showed me a dot on the screen so that I would go through with the abortion."

Wow! So even the abortionists know that those are children and they are still going through with it. Now that's a lie. Oh, that's right. Who's the father of all lies? Satan. Now that's just the first lie. The second lie they tell ladies is don't worry, don't be scared, it won't hurt at all. Really? Well, that's not what the ladies experienced. Let's take a look at this one.

"I remember them inserting some kind of vacuum and then this loud noise came on."

"They turned on the vacuum machine and it was a loud horrible noise. "

"The sound of that vacuum machine, I'll never forget that noise."

"The sound of the vacuum extracting the baby."

"As they began the procedure my body felt like it was being violently shaken off the table. They were yelling at me to be still. Tears were streaming down my face."

"The sound of this machine was like a ghoulish generator. Then the pain hit me."

"I've never felt something so painful and so awful as that procedure."

"It was excruciating, the pain."

"It was excruciatingly painful. I almost passed out."

"I asked for a double Valium that they offered to give us to calm our nerves, but it wasn't enough to subdue the pain."

"The kind psychiatrist that gave me the advice turned into a very cold, cold, calculating abortionist. Basically, he said, you will feel a little tug and it will hurt a little bit and that's it. Well, it was much more than that. It was the feeling of my child being ripped from my body."

"And immediately the tears started rolling down my eyes. I was regretful at that instance. But it was too late for me to say anything or to do anything."

"I don't think anything hurt as much as my heart and soul hurt at that moment. Because lying on that table I realized what they were doing, and it was too late to stop. They sucked the life right out of my body. I knew I would never be able to get back."

"How could something that is a woman's right cause so much pain."

"And I knew right then and there, I knew I had made the biggest mistake of my life."

"I tried to sit up to see what was going on and she pushed me back down and put her back to me with her hand on my chest. I kept trying to get up because I wanted to see, and she took a pillow and put it on top of me again to block my view. I saw her pick up a trash can and then again, she was trying to almost straddle me to keep me from seeing, but at that time I saw a nurse come in at another angle and she was carrying a trash bag and then my mother gasped and said, 'Oh my gosh, it's twins.' And I heard one nurse say to the other nurse. 'It's twins.' And then she took the trash bag and she tied it in a knot, and she walked out. I can see it just as clear as day, she walked out with the twins in that trash bag."

"The nurse looked up at me and smiling said, 'Oh look, twins.' I can remember screaming. Oh my God what have I done? Then I began to scream, stop, stop! I was trying to get up off the table and the abortionist began to scream at me to lay still and the nurse had to come and put her body over mine to hold me down."

Satan gets you to buy into the doubt, then here comes the lie, and every one of those ladies, as soon as the procedure starts, they realized they were duped but it was too late. But satan keeps going. What does he say? You know what, it's just harmless. It's harmless, you'll be fine. Don't worry about it. This procedure not only murders the children, it destroys the woman's body. Take a look at this

"Two days after the abortion, I was sitting at the place where I lived, and I started cramping severely. So, I went into the bathroom, to go to the bathroom and when I went to wipe myself it felt as though I had passed something. When I looked down, in my hand was my baby. I remember seeing the hands and the feet, the skin was translucent, a tiny little thing, and the eyes were forming. I was so horrified that I dropped the baby and flushed the toilet because I couldn't imagine that that was what I had just seen. I ran to the phone to call the abortion facility to tell them what happened and all they had to say to me was 'Well, that's too bad.' Then they hung up on me.

"Pieces of my child had actually been left inside of me. I had developed an infection which led to bleeding. My doctor proceeded to tell me that I could have died from the infection, I could have bled to death or he might have had to

perform a hysterectomy in which I could never have had children. I was only 18 years old."

"The caller-ID said that Laura was calling. We were always so happy to hear from her. She was such a joy. When I answered the phone, I didn't hear Laura's voice. I heard screaming and crying. I could make out four words. Laura not breathing, emergency room, and abortion. I immediately called the hospital and finally got the doctor in the ER to talk to me. He was telling me everything that they did for Laura. How hard they worked on her. I kept praying the whole time. God give her a chance. Then the doctor got to the end of the sentence and he said two words that hit me like thunder. He said, 'She's gone.' The oxygen was sucked out of my room when she said those words. We got there at two o'clock in the morning. Laura was brought down to the morgue. I had not led a sheltered life, but nothing prepared me for this. To see my beautiful daughter wheeled in on a gurney, in a body bag. He unzipped the body bag and inside was laying my beautiful daughter with all the tubes still attached to her."

"I'm a nurse and I worked in the intensive care unit. A few years back a young girl came to our hospital with her boyfriend. She had just had an abortion two days prior and she was bleeding very badly with a fever. She was taken to surgery immediately and ended up with a hysterectomy. She was also brought into our intensive care unit after her surgery and eventually she passed away. As the parents came to the hospital, I watched the father lay across his daughter's bed weeping, that he would never hear her voice, or talk to his daughter again."

It looks pretty harmful to me. Satan not only got them to kill their own child, but ladies die because of this. If somehow, they do survive, there are all kinds of physical complications that they don't go on to tell you. Let me give you a list. As a result of abortion, murdering your child, you run the risk of hemorrhage requiring transfusion, perforation of the uterus, cardiac arrest, endotoxic shock, major unintended surgery resulting in hospitalization, convulsions, undiagnosed tubal pregnancy, cervical lacerations, uterine rupture and death, as you just saw in two occurrences. This is from medical journals. Why isn't this being put out in the news? Abortion can increase your risk for breast cancer. Hasn't that been on the increase for quite a few decades? What has also been around for the last several decades? Abortion, do you think there is a link there? Maybe it's milk, or maybe it's ..., or maybe it's this. From a medical journal, a review of twenty-three cases of breast cancer and abortion, they identified seventeen of those studies indicated an increase of breast cancer among those women who had had abortions. So, seventeen out of twenty-three are going to get breast cancer. That's a pretty high number. So much for being harmless. But, satan, he's a liar. That's what he does. And he wants murder, whether it be a child, or you. He keeps going, he's not satisfied. The next thing he tells ladies, 'Hey, listen, I'll tell you what. Maybe you think it was a baby, whatever, but don't worry. You can have babies later.' Really? A lot of them that go through this procedure are not going to have kids. Listen to these ladies.

"I got married at 20 years old and shortly after that I decided to have children. And as time went on, I wasn't able to conceive. I went to a doctor to find out why. I was then told that because of all the scar tissue that was in my uterus, because of my choice of abortion, that I would probably never be able to conceive a child. I ended up having twelve surgeries, laparoscopies, DNC's, fertility drugs. I had about four to five miscarriages. All due to the choice that I made, two or three years prior to that."

"I went to the doctors to have a laparoscopy and a dye test. They showed me on the screen that my tubes were blocked. It was from the suction of the machine from the abortions. One of my tubes was 90% blocked, the other one was 100% blocked."

"The doctor told me that because of all that scarring in my uterus, from the abortions, that I had been left infertile. And that most likely I would not become pregnant again."

"I laid on the table and started thinking, how am I going to tell my husband that I'm not going to be able to have children with him. It was the reality of knowing that the only three children I would ever bear, I killed."

Isn't that another thing that is on the rise? Not only the increase of breast cancer but infertility has gone crazy. Wonder why? See if you can guess who this is. This is an actual testimony.

"I had an abortion at 17 and it was the worst thing I ever did. I was two months along when I realized it. I went to my mom and she said, 'You have to get rid of it!' She told me where the clinic was and literally pushed me off, she was so angry. She said I got myself in a mess and now she had to get me out. But she didn't come, I went alone. I was terrified. It was full of other young girls and they were all terrified. Everybody was looking at each other and nobody is saying a

word. I got my way through it. I never would recommend it to anyone because it comes back to haunt you. Then when I tried to have children, I lost three and I think it was because something happened to my cervix during the abortion. After three miscarriages they had to put a stitch in it."

That was Sharon Osborne. Ozzy Osborne's wife. Even she admits it. Again, from the medical journals, the growing rates of infertility after a woman has had an abortion, many researchers are reluctant to name surgical abortion as a possible cause or factor. Why? Because abortion is such a controversial issue that any expert who speaks up and links abortion with a negative side effect is regarded as a secret pro-lifer and is in danger of committing professional suicide. Interesting choice of words. Such a scientist or researcher risks being shunned by colleagues and ridiculed by the media in professional journals. So, they know it, but they aren't going to do it because they don't want the word to get out.

Now for some proof. West African women involved in eleven issues of infertility lasting from anywhere from 2 to 15 years duration, all these women had a previous abortion between 10 and 26 weeks of gestation. What they found out was they had retained pieces of fetal baby bones and tissue inside of them. Hysteroscopy was performed to remove the bone fragments and then 8 out of 11 women subsequently were able to conceive. In other words, there were still baby parts inside the woman that was keeping them from getting pregnant. Some of the women, once they were removed, were able to conceive, while others still couldn't. In a first trimester abortion, the doctor performs what is called an incomplete abortion, sometimes accidently leaving some tissue in the uterus. (We saw before that sometimes it's not accidental, sometimes, remember that one guy, he stopped because he thought the baby was further along. He said he wasn't going to continue until they gave him more money.)

When the baby tissue is left inside the womb, it can rot, and it can cause severe infection. It can cause permanent damage to the female reproductive organs or can cause sterility or miscarriage of future pregnancies. Also, they run the risk of infection, pelvic inflammatory disease or PID which is inflammation of the uterus, fallopian tubes and the ovaries. Also the uses of the instruments that they use, not only the vacuum, just for the first trimester, when the baby gets bigger they can't suck it out, they have to use the devices to literally rip the baby apart, limb by limb, arm by arm, piece by piece, part by part, and what that does is it not only further spreads infection, and it can further damage the internal sides as well. A Scandinavian study found that women with a previous PID had a decrease in fertility following the abortion and, in some cases, multiple abortions caused scarring on top of the cervix or inside the uterus. Any procedure that dilates the cervix, which is a necessary step for most abortions, can weaken it, and can affect the ability of the embryo to implant into the uterus or the ability of your cervix to support the pregnancy.

In other words, you aren't going to get pregnant anymore. It destroys your insides. Also, because of abortion, this is often used to fulfill this goal, delaying childbearing. You know why? What is the lie of feminism, who started that lie, who is the father of lies? But what is the lie of feminism? Children are bad, children are a nuisance, so is getting married and families. And for you weak ladies who eventually, unfortunately, crack, and you don't get out there and prove that you can do everything a man can do, then, okay, later you can do it. Well, see, that is the lie. First of all, what does the Bible say about children? Children are a blessing from God. Children are a gift from God. Blessed is the man whose quiver is full. The scripture is very clear about that. Marriage, is that a torment? It's a gift from God. Procreation, that's a gift from God. It comes with marriage by the way. But the lie of feminism and the abortion industry is, go ahead and wait, you can wait, do your career, whatever, you can wait. Try to be a man all you want. Later you can have it. No. What happens with that lie, they're saying, is that not only are you damaged by the abortion, sometimes you die, but it also says, ladies, the older you get, the less chances and you are pushing it further away, you are decreasing your natural chances by age. But in order to delay the childbearing guess what they are using as a form of birth control? Abortion. That's the whole point of what they are saying.

Another point is what they call the estrogen connection. A growing body of scientific evidence suggests that while a number of factors may be to blame in the rising number of infertility rates, the greatest could be the excess of estrogen. An excess of estrogen hormone can affect ovulation in women and some experts believe that uterine fibroids, endometriosis, ovarian cists, and infections of the reproductive organs, all of which can impair fertility in women, are often the result of estrogen overload. Here is where I am going with this. What do you think the body produces when you get pregnant? Many experts will agree that the excess estrogen can be the cause or factor for infertility. Most would avoid all suggestions that abortion may also be a contributing cause because of all the politics involved. They don't want to talk about that. In a 7-8-week gestation, a pregnant woman's blood already contains 6 time more estrogen than at the time of conception. More than twice the level contained in the non-pregnant state.

What they are saying is, you are continually getting pregnant, you may have several abortions in a year, when you get several abortions your estrogen levels are spiking on a constant basis. You ask, how do they get it to go down? After the pregnancy, you carry it to term, many women breast-feed and that suppresses the production of estrogen. See how God has it all designed? When the baby is born, then you breast-feed, which makes the estrogen level go down. But what are these ladies doing with abortion? You are getting repeatedly pregnant, but you have no way for those levels to go back down because you're killing your children. You don't have a chance to breast-feed to lower the estrogen levels.

Let me give you a couple more. Satan says "I know you're getting concerned at this point, but just trust me he says, you'll be fine. Your life will turn out great." Really? I don't think so. Listen to what these ladies have to say.

"The grief and trauma and shame, that we as women deal with, with this choice, I wouldn't wish on my worst enemy."

"When I walked out of that clinic and I walked down Santa Monica Blvd., I knew I was a different person. I felt like there was something evil inside of me. I felt like I could do anything and there were no boundaries anymore. I felt murderous. I felt unloving and uncompassionate."

"I didn't realize that, after that, I would have these kinds of complications, and that I would really be struggling emotionally. They didn't tell me any of that. I wish somebody had."

"I remember putting on my mask, going to church, crying myself to sleep every night, in your arms, (as she looks at her husband) and we would just justify it and say that we did what we had to do. But for 12 years that went on."

"I began wearing a mask to hide the shame and guilt of what I had done. I began partying and nightclub drinking to the point where I would get falling down drunk. I used illegal drugs, anything that I could use to numb the pain that I was in."

"So, I went back to school, pretended like it didn't happen. But I started drinking and smoking some pot. And trying to get rid of the pain that was so deep."

"I just remember I was doing a lot of partying and a lot of drinking, even experimenting with certain drugs."
"I became very promiscuous, I was drinking more, taking drugs."

"I immediately started to drink. I used drugs."

"I began to drink more. I used more drugs."

"I began to live at the bars, drinking heavily, doing drugs, being very sexually active."

"I started drinking. I started doing drugs, and I became very promiscuous."

"I was very promiscuous because I had no self-worth. I didn't believe that I had any self-love."

"I hated myself."

"I knew deep inside of me that what I had done was to take the life of my own child."

"I was drowning in this party atmosphere just to numb myself from the pain I was feeling, that I had taken the life of my own baby."

"I felt empty, and I would cry. I couldn't understand my feelings. This was my right to do this. All the feminists said it's my life, it's my body, my right, this was going to help me. Why didn't I feel that way?"

"As time went on, I felt more and more empty and I tried more and more things to try to fill it up. More drugs, more work, more accomplishments, another degree at school, increasingly dysfunctional relationships."

"I went through angry spells where I hated men or I hated myself, or I hated other people."

"I was in a downward spiral of self-destruction that lasted years."

"They said my life would get back to normal again. It's never been back to normal again."

"I just felt shame. I felt guilt. I would grieve, and I grieved for my two children that I wanted so desperately, and I know I can never have. I wanted to meet them and see what they looked like. Hear their voices. And I never gave them a chance to live. And I live with this every single day."

No, you're not fine! And they know it. 100% of the time. You're not fine. It brings all kinds of problems. Data suggests that abortion causes deterioration in mental health. Here are other side effects of abortion i.e. murdering a child. Regret, anger, guilt, shame, feelings of loneliness, isolation, loss of self-confidence, insomnia, nightmares, you can go into some of the ladies' accounts of them dreaming about their babies coming back saying, 'Why did you kill me?' They are tormented every night. Relationship issues, they can't keep a relationship, it's hard to get close, they don't want to get close to a guy. If they do have children later, if they can have children, it messes up that relationship. They are constantly feeling guilty. Eating disorders, is that on the rise? Depression, anxiety, PTSD. Is that on the rise? Suicidal thoughts and feelings. Listen to this, ladies that have an abortion are 110% more likely to abuse alcohol, which we just saw. They are 155% more likely to commit suicide, they are 220% more likely to abuse marijuana. Why? Because they know it was wrong and it is tearing them up on the inside and they are trying to drown the pain out. So much for it being a great thing for your life. That's a lie. Ladies are being lied to; children are being murdered. Ladies are being lied to just like the first woman, they are being deceived by the great deceiver.

Let me give you another one. They say you'll just move on in life, I know it's hard right now, but you will forget about the whole thing. Really? Some ladies can't take the pain anymore. And they make another mistake.

"I was so numb inside and full of self-loathing, just deeply depressed and it finally got to a point where I no longer wanted to live, I felt I could no longer go on."

"I began to have suicidal thoughts and I made a suicide attempt."

"I remember pouring a whole bottle of valium in my hand and a whole bottle of Librium in my hand, and I don't know how many aspirin I poured in my hand because I felt like I was just completely out of control. I can remember taking them all."

"I was listening to depressing music. I was in a pit and I could not get out. I even

tried to kill myself. I turned the gas on in the oven and thank God a friend came to the door. I tried two other times to kill myself as well. My life was out of control."

"After these five abortions I began asking myself, what am I doing? What am I doing? And I started to realize that I was on this merry go round of self-destruction and feeling like I couldn't get off. That it had to stop. I could see that it was almost as though there was a spirit of death, a spirit of destruction that was not only having control over my life but that a spirit was living inside of me and becoming who I was."

Suicide. This again is from a study in Finland. Suicide after an abortion is a lot more common than in the general population. In fact, so much so that the suicide rate after an abortion was three times the general suicide rate. It triples it. As we saw 155% are more likely to kill themselves. Why? Because you have violated a biblical rule. You reap what you sow. Murder, including the murder of a child is a sin. 100% of the time what will sin do to a person? Sin hurts, sin harms, sin destroys. And that is what we see here.

Let me give you one more. Satan's lie says, "Hey listen, it's all about you." Remember Eve? When she was just about to bite the apple, what did her mindset turn to? Me! Food, that's what I like, it's pleasing to the eye, it's going to give me wisdom and stature, right? That is what satan says. "It's about you. Don't you understand? We are making this available to you, the mass murder of children, on demand, because it's all about you!" Women's rights? I don't think so. Let's take a look at what they are actually doing to women.

Ronald Reagan: *"Abortion is advocated only by persons who have themselves been born."*

Jane Brennan author "Motherhood Interrupted" *"These feminist groups do not care about women; they care about abortion. And we need to start talking about this. We need to start asking all of our pro-abortion friends, family members, colleagues, politicians, why do women need abortions? Don't you understand all the trauma that we suffer because of this? All the depression, the suicide attempts, the alcohol and drug abuse, the infertility and even the death. Women are dying from their so-called legal right to choose."*

Man on Video: *"Sin starts the same way every time. It starts with a lie. It's not really a human being. You can do this and forget about it. It's a simple procedure and it won't have any effect. You don't really love the girl you got pregnant. You don't want to marry her; you are doing her a service by paying for this abortion. But sin is not satisfied with the lie, because the lies aim is ownership. Just as all sin, when we engage in the sin, the aim is to own us. Because with ownership comes its true aim and that is destruction. The woman on the table who has the abortion, despite all the lies of our culture, knows what she has done. And that knowledge will destroy her, but for the intervening Grace of God."*

And that's the key. So, odds are, those of you reading this book, you may have fallen for this lie and have actually gone through this yourself. I've got family members that have fallen for this lie. But that is where the grace of God comes into play. You don't need to take drugs. You don't need to act like it didn't happen. You most certainly don't need to make another mistake and kill yourself. You don't need to destroy yourself with even more sexual immorality. You do what you do with any and all sin and you come to Jesus. You own up to it and ask Him to forgive you. The scripture says, if you confess your sins,

John 1:9, "He is faithful and just to forgive of our sins and cleans us from all unrighteousness."

That's what these ladies need. That's what will counter the lie. And the truth, not only for those who might be contemplating that, but unfortunately those who have already fallen for the lie. That is what we need to share with them as well. The feminists and Planned Parenthood are going along with this lie that came from satan. But not just them. Guess who else is going along with it? In fact, they are making it their campaign. It's the Democrat Party. They too say that they are here for women. We're here for children. We're here for families. Real needs for real people. We're here to guarantee your right for abortion. And what we saw, straight from the ladies' mouth, is that really helping ladies? No, it's killing children and destroying lives. Whole families, it's destroying our society. And as we saw the chart before, in the biggest historical plot of people running as a Democratic Candidate in this upcoming presidential election, there is not one pro-lifer. Not one! In fact, one of the new guys they are popping back on, though he lied and said he wasn't going to run but now he's running, is Mr. Beto O'Rourke. Here's what he said, remember he is supposed to be for women, and families, and children. Here's what he said in a recent interview.

Reporter: "*Are you for a third trimester abortion? Or are you going to protect the lives of third trimester babies? Because there is not really a medical necessity for abortion, there's not a medical emergency procedure and typically a third trimester abortion takes up to three days to have. So, in that sense if there was an emergency the doctors would just do a C-section and you wouldn't have to kill the baby. So, are you for or against a third trimester abortion?*"

Beto O'Rourke: "*The question is about abortion and reproduction rights and my answer to you is, that should be the decision that the woman makes...*"

And they cheered their own destruction. On the life of children. I said it before, and I will say it again. That's always the throwback. He didn't answer the question. He reworded it and said it's all about a woman's right to choose. I'm sorry, but no woman and no man have the right to choose to kill a child. But that is the ruse that is being played. Now you know why I keep saying that the Democrat Party has turned into the Death Party. And based on what we have seen so far, they are the women and children destroyer party. Don't you want to vote for them? I don't think so. You can also call them the Molech supporters. Because that is what is really going on. History is repeating itself. We have a whole political party in our own country that is supporting that. Why? Because they have fallen for a lie. They are lying too. And who's the father of all lies? Satan. Next chapter we are going to get into the response to abortion. When those people come up to us, like the Democrats that are for abortion, how do you respond to that? How do you come back biblically, philosophically and factually? How do you not fall for their web of deceit? Remember they use terminology to get you off target. How do we witness to those people?

Chapter Six

The Response to Abortion

Now we are going to get into the response. Because you and I can see and believe, rightly so, biblically, philosophically and logically, that this is wrong, murdering children is wrong. I can't even believe we are having a discussion about this, but we have a large element of our society that says, "Oh, no, I not only believe it's my right, but you can't tell me to stop." How do you reason with those people? How do we respond? Well, we do it the biblical way and we give a reasonable defense. And that is what we will see in our opening text. Do we just not say anything? Like, I can't talk to you because it makes me mad? That doesn't help. We need to speak up even though it might get a little bit heated, it doesn't need to be heated. You don't need to be eye for an eye, tooth for a tooth, but if anything, speak up on behalf of what you know. If you don't speak up, you know what is going to happen. A child is going to be murdered. So, give it a defense.

I Peter 3:15, 16 "But in your hearts set apart Christ as Lord. *(Once in a while? No. Just those people who have memorized the whole Bible? No. Just Pastors, because we expect them to have all the answers? No, what does it say?)* Always be prepared to give an answer *('always' be prepared to give an answer to everyone you meet, even the people that believe in murdering children, yes.)* to everyone who asks you to give the reason for the hope that you have. But do this with gentleness and respect. *(It's not eye for an eye or tooth for a tooth, that doesn't help anything.)* keeping a clear conscience so that those who speak maliciously against your good behavior in Christ may be ashamed of their slander."

We've already seen that that is oftentimes a powerful way to witness to people. You have seen some testimonies already of people who have worked at abortion clinics or ran abortion clinics, but a Christian came in there and stood up and gave a defense and did so lovingly and respectfully. What happened? People got saved and they quit doing what they were doing, i.e. murdering children. So that is what we are going to deal with in this chapter. To give a biblical, philosophical, logical response on why it is wrong to murder children. We are going to take a look at a lot of things that they throw back to you and I and then we are going to begin to answer them.

The first thing they say is, "What's the big deal, why are you making a big case out of this, because it doesn't hurt anybody." Excuse me? It doesn't hurt anybody? You just killed a baby! But that is typically what they will say. In fact, it's a pathway to destruction. Let me give you some statistics: There are around one million abortions taking place annually just in the United States. Every year on average, one million children are being murdered in our country. Does that hurt anybody? Sure, a million or more. And we don't even know if we have the right numbers. I didn't realize this until I came across this one. There is a problem with the reporting methods. Some states don't report, including California, at certain times. So, do we have a true figure? We are saying 60 plus million but maybe it's a lot more. We don't know. More than 25% of abortions are the chemical, saline salt, solution where they burn the child, inside and out, waiting for it to die and then you deliver it. Does that hurt anybody? Nearly 75% are surgical, that is when they rip them apart. Does that hurt anybody? 41% of women who have had abortions in the U.S. had no other children. We saw where that leads to infertility. Does that hurt anybody? Remember, that is the premise, it doesn't hurt anybody. 44% of women that had abortions in the U.S. had a previous abortion. So now it is a pattern of behavior, which destroys them. Did that hurt anybody? 86% of women who had abortions in the U.S. were unmarried. Again, maybe if you do it God's way then you wouldn't be in this situation. But still, if you are in that situation, there is no reason for you to kill a child.

I will say this, ladies, if you have a guy that is pressuring you to not do it God's way, i.e. wait until marriage, you need to dump him, he's a klutz. If he professes to be a Christian, he's not the kind of Christian you want to marry. Because if he is going to do that before you get married what do you think is going to happen afterwards? Even if he is at the point that he says he's a Christian and he is trying to get you to go through with an abortion, dump him! You can always put the baby up for adoption. Why does the baby have to die for something it did not do?

41% of abortions are among women and teens 24 years old and younger. Remember, they are using the schools as the harvest grounds, via sex education. 40% of minors have abortions and their parents know nothing about it. Is that good for family relations? Encouraging kids to lie to the parents? Is that hurting anybody? It is estimated that 25% of American women will have an abortion by the age of 45. 25% of all women in our country, statistically, are going to have their life destroyed. But again, what is the premise? It's not going to hurt anybody. Also, ladies are using it as a form of contraception, 34% of all abortions were repeats. Here are the reasons given for getting an abortion:

4% said they would interfere with their education or career.
7% said they weren't mature enough to raise a child.
8% said they don't want to be a single mother.
19% said they were done having children.
23% said they can't afford a baby.

Last time I checked all babies cost money. You who are trying to talk about this decision about killing the baby, did you know that you cost your parents? Aren't you glad they paid for you?

25% say they are not ready for a child.

Then get out of the bedroom. And again, ladies, if you are getting pressured, dump them. Do it God's way and you can avoid the whole thing.

Now, whose got the highest rates? The District of Columbia, Washington D.C., 38% of pregnancies end in the murder of a child. Do you think that reflects our capital, our nation? New York State, 33%, New Jersey, 30%, all end in abortion. Black women were more than 3 ½ times more likely to have an abortion than white women. Do you not think there is eugenics going on here? Of course, it is. Margaret Sanger's dream is still being put into action. The abortion rate of women with Medicaid is 3 times as high as other women. Why? We are going to see that they get government funding, via Medicaid, but also, they prey on the poor. Remember what Margaret Sanger said? The poor, the blacks, the non-Caucasian, are misfits, they are morons, and they need to be gotten rid of like weeds.

30% of women who aborted their child said they were Protestant. 30%, not 3%, and it should be 0%. Sounds like the church is a little confused on this issue. No wonder we are doing this study. But remember, it doesn't hurt anybody. That was our first premise. The total number of abortions in the U.S. is now over 61 million and again it may be higher because some states don't always report. About 25% of all children in the United States are murdered. 219 abortions per 1,000 live births. Just in the United States, every 30 seconds a child is murdered. Remember it doesn't hurt anybody. Globally, around the world, 25% of pregnancies around the whole planet end in abortion. It's one thing to read these statistics, let me show you what it looks like. This is what we need to be aware of. You can go online and type in 'abortion clock' and you can see how many children are being murdered around the world, it's mind-blowing!

USAbortionClock.org

In United States today

1,729.3

US since 1973: Roe vs Wade

61,238,542.7

By Planned Parenthood since 1970

8,397,639.5

By Planned Parenthood this year

109,394.0

United States this Year

296,509.7

US this Year after 16 weeks gestation

14,232.5

US this Year due to rape or incest

2,876.1

Black babies since '73 in US

18,371,562.8

Worldwide since 1980

1,532,705,318

Worldwide this Year

12,856,900

WW since you loaded this page

54

Worldwide Today

74,085

Now this was a Monday, about ten in the morning and you can see well over a thousand children were murdered just by ten in the morning. If you go online, you can see that it will still be clicking away. Just this year we have aborted over a quarter of a million children in our country. Black babies since 1973, 18,000,000+, and again, you don't think that eugenics is involved? Since

1980, worldwide, that is 1.53 billion children and worldwide, in just three months 12,856,900 and if you are looking at this online, it is about 1 abortion every second, not 30 seconds, every second around the world. Oh, but remember what they said. It doesn't hurt anyone. You are going to stand before God on that one. So, that's one thing that we can demonstrate.

The second thing that they say is, "You know what, it doesn't affect you. It's my belief, leave me alone, just back off." Let's see if we can examine that. One way that it does affect us is financially. Planned Parenthood is not a multi-million-dollar corporation, it is a multi-*billion*-dollar corporation. States use public funds to pay for abortions, which means our tax dollars are going to fund abortions, i.e. the murder of children. So, yes it does affect me. As a taxpayer, that's not right. Planned Parenthood has historically stated that, "Oh no, we don't use those funds for abortions." That's a lie. So, lets respond to that. Here's the facts. Do our taxpayer dollars pay for abortions at Planned Parenthood?

Cecile Richards, President of Planned Parenthood: *"No Federal funds pay for abortion services at Planned Parenthood." "That's exactly right, Federal Funding does not go to abortion services at Planned Parenthood." "Federal Funding as you probably know does not pay for abortion services."*

Don't be misled!

Live Actions News: *"Many people think that none of our taxpayer dollars go to pay for abortions, but nothing could be further from the truth. Planned Parenthood is America's largest abortion chain.*

Over 320,000 abortions a year.
887 abortions a day.

Yet every year Planned Parenthood gets over half a billion dollars in state and federal taxpayer funding which averages to over $1.5 million a day."

In an attempt to defend themselves, Planned Parenthood states over and over again in their talking points that according to the Hyde Amendment: No, federal dollars cannot pay for abortions in most cases, but keep in mind that amendment only covers federal funding of abortion, not state funding of abortion. 17 states, covering about 40% of the U.S. population use taxpayer dollars to pay for abortions in programs such as Medicaid.

When you call Planned Parenthood in one of these states you hear something like this. 'You sound like, actually, a perfect candidate for Medicaid. And they do cover terminations in full.' So, a portion of Planned Parenthoods $554 million in government revenue comes directly from state taxpayer funded abortions.

But federal taxpayer dollars also pay for abortions. Under the Federal Program Title X your federal taxpayer dollars directly pay for potential abortion inducing emergency contraception, such as Plan B and the Morning After Pill. Additionally, the Hyde Amendment is insufficient to stop federal funding to pay for Planned Parenthood abortion business because money is fungible.

The concept of fungibility is this. Let's say 16-year-old, Stacy, wants to buy a New Big Screen TV that cost $1,000.00. Stacy has $1,000.00 but she has to save $500.00 to fix her car. Her mom comes along and says 'I'll give you $500.00 to fix the car but it is only for the car. No way am I giving you money to buy a TV, in fact I am only going to reimburse you after you get the car fixed. Obviously, because of mom, Stacy now has enough money to fix her car and buy the TV.

Fungibility means that even though mom kept her money from directly paying for the TV she still helped Stacy pay for it by freeing up Stacy's other money. The same is true for Planned Parenthood. They do things like abortions, birth control, STD testing, marketing and lobbying and they fund these with millions and millions of dollars in income and donations. So, when the government comes along and gives Planned Parenthood hundreds of millions of our taxpayers dollars a year, even though it is technically restricted, it frees up that donation money to pay for their abortion operations, including procedures, facilities, staffing, building costs and other abortion overhead expenses. As former Planned Parenthood manager, Sue Thayer says, 'It's all one big pot.'

Sue Thayer, *former Planned Parenthood Manager: "You picture one big pot. All the money comes into the pot because there weren't separate abortion facilities. It was a contraceptive clinic with an abortion facility in it. There is no possible way to keep that money separate."*

"To use specific examples, when Planned Parenthood receives taxpayer money through Title X, that money can pay for the physicians and clinicians that assist with the abortion in the same facility that the abortions are committed.

In fact, call up a taxpayer funded Planned Parenthood facility and ask for an abortion and this is what you get. 'We tell you you're pregnant and then we offer at Planned Parenthood to do the abortions.' 'We only offer pregnancy test, and then abortion care if that's what you wanted to go with.' 'It will be $715; we do offer limited financial assistance. It is based on your, um, household size and income.' 'We do abortions here, but like, with the three options, I guess, I could do an abortion in the clinic, but the other two options I would have to go outside of Planned Parenthood?'

'Right. Uh-huh. Yep'

Live Action News: *"So when taxpayer money does fund abortion facilitators, and does fund abortion facilities, how can anyone make the claim the federal taxpayer money does not fund abortions? If we take a look at these numbers over time, we see that government funding has increased and so have Planned Parenthoods' abortions. Especially in the last 15 years. Notice how the slopes in*

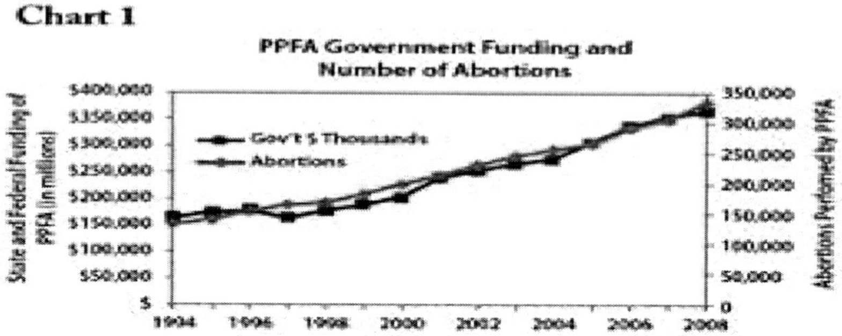

the graphs have a similar shape.

Planned Parenthood says defunding them would deprive many people from basic healthcare. But that is completely up to Planned Parenthood. Understand that Planned Parenthood always has the option of keeping their ½ billion dollars in taxpayer money if they shut down the business, but they refuse the option."

Ari Shapiro, NPR: *"President Trump says funding will flow in full, if Planned Parenthood just agrees to stop performing abortions. Would you ever?"*

Cecile Richards: *"Absolutely not."*

Wow. You don't want to stop the murder because that is where you are making millions of dollars. And did you notice the little financial game that they play? We are funding this as taxpayers. Half a billion per year. Did you catch that? 1 ½ million dollars per day of our tax dollars are going to what? Murder children. But hey, they said it doesn't affect us, no big deal. But let's explore that further.

What about the long-term effect of murdering children on our society? Think of all the doctors that will never be born. Maybe one of them had the actual cure for cancer. It's not going to happen now, you killed him. Think about it. The effects on society when you continue to murder what could have been the next generation. What about all the businessmen and women, what about all the pastors and preachers, and teachers, and what effects are being done on your society by these people who will never be, because you killed them that could have been a positive output for our society? So yes, it does affect us. In fact, would you consider an abortion in the following situations? Here are four cases. And they are all true stories by the way:

1. There's a preacher and wife who are very, very, poor and they had 14 kids. Now she finds out she's pregnant with her 15th. They are living in tremendous poverty. Considering their poverty and the excessive world population, would you consider recommending she get an abortion?

2. The father is sick, the mother has T.B., they have 4 children, the first one is blind, the second one just died, the third one is deaf, and the 4th one came down with T.B. She finds out she is pregnant again. Given the extreme situation would you consider recommending she get an abortion?

3. A white man raped a 13-year-old black girl and she got pregnant. If you were her parents would you consider recommending an abortion?

4. A teenage girl is pregnant, and she isn't married. Her fiancé isn't the father of the baby and he is upset. Would you consider recommending an abortion?

Well, if you did, remember the effects on society. In the first case if you said yes you just killed John Wesley, one of the greatest evangelists of the 19th century. If you said yes in the second case, you just killed Beethoven. In the third case if you said yes you just killed Ethel Waters, a great black gospel singer. And in the fourth case if you said yes, you just declared the murder of Jesus Christ.

There is never a case for abortion. And it affects us in a major way. In some ways that we may never know. Only God knows.

Then they push on a little bit further and they say it doesn't affect you Christians. "Why do you Christians get so hung up on this? Just back off, go into your little bubble and we won't bug you with this." Well, that's not true. There is no bubble, it's gone beyond just bugging us, to use that term. There is talk in our country right now of forcing churches to pay for abortions. Let me give you one example. Washington state to churches, '*Pay for abortions or break the law.*' The attorneys for a church in Seattle filed a federal lawsuit on Friday against Washington state officials for forcing churches to pay for abortions in their health care insurance. Take a look:

CBN News reports: "*Joining us now from the Alliance Defending Freedom as the firm representing the Seattle church is Kevin Theriot, so what more can you tell us about this case?*"

Kevin Theriot Alliance Defending Freedom: "*This case is really about the state trying to force churches to act contrary to their religious convictions. Of course, churches should not be forced to fund abortions, and this is exactly what this law does.*"

CBN News reports: "*Do you think this case shows a double standard regarding religious liberty and separation of church and state?*"

Kevin Theriot: "*Certainly it does, this is the government intruding on the affairs of the church and not only the churches, but all religious organizations are forced to fund abortion in violation of their convictions. A church shouldn't be required to include abortion when in its health care provision for its employees, just because it covers maternity.*"

CBN News reports: "*So what makes the churches be required to include abortion coverage in health care?*"

Kevin Theriot: "*Well, they mistakenly believe that abortion is a part of health care, but abortion is not health care. They of course think that abortion is vital in* *order for a woman to be able to be successful and that is completely contrary. Many women in our organization and in our church believe that women can have successful lives and we can protect women through childbearing without forcing them or coercing them to participate in an abortion."*

CBN News Reports: "*So Kevin what is the end goal in this case? What are you hoping to achieve?"*

Kevin Theriot: "*Well we want to get this law struck down because it coerces churches to violate their religious convictions."*

Cedar Park spokesman: *"This law requires pro-life churches to violate their religious convictions about life and have their insurance plan fund abortions. Cedar Park church believes that abortion is not health care.*

A couple from CP Church: *"What we are defending and standing for are the rights of people of faith to not be forced into being complicit about something that is inconsistent with our faith."*

Cedar Park Spokesman: *"The churches health care insurance is intended to protect life, to help mothers that are welcoming a new baby into the world. Not to end life through abortion."*

A couple from CP Church: *"We distinctly do not cover abortion. It's who we are as an organization, what our beliefs are, how we live out our faith."*

CBN News Reports: "*And the costs to not obey this law?"*

Cedar Park Spokesman: "*The violation of this law would not only mean that the church would face fines, but actual prison time."*

So much for not affecting the Christian. And apparently our tax dollars, as Christians, the 1 ½ million you get per day is not enough. Now you want it to be in Medicare. You want to make sure there is no excuse for people to come to your murder mill and help you become a millionaire. Oh, by the way, and this is in Washington state, the bill's sponsor is a Democrat State Senator, Steve Hobbs. Once again, I call them the Death Party. The bill had a lack of religious exemptions, so everybody has to comply, including churches. He declined to change it, saying this: '*Employers have the option of suing.*' In other words, sue me if you don't like it. Then he said, *'Health care is about the individual, not about them.'* Well, who are them? Christians! So now you are saying a baby is not a baby, which is a lie, and apparently a Christian is not an individual. Folks, this is where it is going. And you wonder why we need to speak up.

Don't us their terminology. You've heard me say this repeatedly. I have given you a couple of examples, but I am going to give you many more. Don't use their terminology because they hide behind it. Their terminology avoids the issue, escapes the issue, tries to soften the issue or silence the issue. No, you need to rephrase it in a biblical, real manner. Let me give you the first example.

They say it is a fetus. You are arguing over a fetus. No, I'm arguing over a baby. Sometimes they will say a blob of tissue or even say a parasite. Yet it has been medically proven that the baby in the womb feels pain. It's not a parasite. It's not a blob of tissue. We know, and they know, scientifically, why are you hiding the sonogram? We all know it's a baby. So, stop using this fake term fetus, it's a baby, it's a child from the moment of conception. Even the secular science channel came out with a video of birth from the beginning when the egg is fertilized at conception and grows to develop a spine, then a tiny beating heart, then the eyes develop, and the arms and legs with fingers and toes, pretty soon the baby is sucking its thumb while kicking and moving all around. The baby can smile, and yawn, suck on its toes, the eyes are opened now, and the baby can see its fingers and toes. After nine months the baby is getting in position to be born. With some struggling to get through the birth canal the baby is born and put in the mother's arms.

"Pregnancy is a process that invites you to surrender to the unseen power behind all of life." And that power is God. And that is a baby.

It's not a blob of tissue. It's not a fetus, it's a baby. Don't get tricked into using that terminology because it's awfully hard for somebody, unless their heart is extremely dark and hard, to sit there and say, "Yes, I'm pro-murdering babies." That's even hard to come off your lips for a normal person. This is from WebMD, which is a secular medical source. Even they admit that life begins at conception. This is right off their website:

The very first page says, '*Your baby, it's growth, you're pregnant, congratulations.*' The very next page, development, month by month, they say, '*Fertilization happens when the sperm meets and penetrates an egg, it's also called conception, at this moment the genetic makeup is complete, including the sex of the baby.'*

They know it's a baby, but they hide behind the term fetus. They just say it's a blob of tissue. It's a lie. Another term they use is 'abortion' and 'Termination of pregnancy.' No, you just murdered a child. That's what it is. Are you against abortion? Yes, I am, I am against murdering children. Phrase it correctly. Because that is really what it is. They say the procedure is just a dilation extraction, i.e. partial birth abortion. That's all it is. No let me explain what is going on here. *"The baby is delivered feet first, the head is left inside the birth canal, a sharp instrument is used to puncture the skull at the base, the brains are then sucked out, then once the baby is dead, it is fully delivered."*

Are you against **Partial Birth Abortion?** Yes, I am against pulling the baby out by its feet, leaving its head in the womb, and sucking its brains out. I'm against that! Because that is what it is. They hide behind the terminology and when you explain that, how do you support that? They say, No, it's just a DNC. Well, let me explain that. The abortionist, i.e. the murderer, inserts a curved knife into the placenta and cuts the baby into pieces before it is suctioned out. You're against a woman's right to a **DNC**? I am against a person using a curved knife into the placenta and cutting the baby into pieces and sucking it out with a vacuum. I'm very much against that! You mean to tell me you are for that? You're going to defend that?

Let me give you another term. **Dilation and Evacuation.** That's when the abortionist inserts a plier-like instrument into the uterus and grabs whatever part of the baby they come in contact with, then they twist and pull until they literally dismember the baby and pull it out piece by piece from the woman until it is killed. Do you mean you are against Dilation and Evacuation? Yes, I am against pulling a baby from inside the womb, by each body part and then stick it on the side of the table. I'm very much against that! You mean to tell me; you are for that? You're out there marching with your signs saying yeah, lets dismember children. Why don't you put that on your sign because that is what you're fighting for! Stop hiding behind the terminology.

Pregnancy reduction. Who could be against that? Well, I am because here's what that is. It is the method of reducing the number of babies in the womb. Can you believe that this actually goes on? Let's say you're not just pregnant, but you are blessed, remember what the Bible says, 'Blessed is the man whose quiver is full of them.' You're blessed with twins or maybe even triplets, but you know what they do? They inject poison into the heart of one or more of the babies while still in the womb. You got blessed with triplets, but you only want one. So, they inject poison into the other two. You're against pregnancy reduction? I am against murdering children and I am certainly against playing favoritism with children and murdering the other two by injecting poison into their hearts. You mean to tell me; you're for that? Wow!

Saline and amniocentesis. That is when they take saline and salt solution and inject it into the placenta. The baby then ingests that dangerous salt solution into the lungs and literally burns the baby alive inside and out. The baby eventually dies, but often times it doesn't, but it does the deed. It burns the baby inside and out and then it's delivered. You're against that? Absolutely! If a person poured hot boiling oil on a child outside of the womb, what would happen to them? They'd go to jail. But it's okay to do something like that inside the womb. I've got a problem with that.

Suction Aspiration. That is a hollow plastic suction tube that is inserted into the placenta and the strong suction tears the baby to pieces and then is sucked out. I'm against that!

Reproductive rights. You're against reproductive rights? Well, first of all, nobody has the right to murder a child. Men, women, I don't care! But you're not producing anything, you're actually killing something. You want killing rights, not reproductive rights. You're not reproducing, you're taking away. The opposite of what you say.

They're hiding behind the terminology. Don't fall for that. Then they make you and I look like the bad guys. And you know how to make somebody look bad? Before their term put the word 'anti.' Who wants to be 'anti'? We aren't only against abortion; we are anti-abortion. I don't care, I'll wear that label because I am anti-murdering children. Who wouldn't be? Because that is what it is. But they use that to make us look bad. Anti-abortion rights or anti-choice, hey, we believe in freedom of choice. Women, you can choose what to wear, what you want to eat, where you want to live, we're not against you making choices, but what we are against is choosing to murder a child. Whether it's a man, a woman, or whoever it is. We're not against choice.

Some people will say the Bible doesn't mention abortion. So, it's ok. Let's follow that logic for a little bit here. Did you know that the Bible does not mention the word Trinity? It doesn't. So, does that mean we can't believe in the Trinity? No, we believe in the Trinity because it's based in the Scripture. Old Testament and New Testament, right? Let us make man in our image, the Genesis account. Who was at Jesus' baptism? God the Father, God the Spirit, and God the Son. The Trinity is all over the scripture. That's why we believe in it. The actual word trinity may not be in the Bible, but if you are going to follow that logic, maybe we shouldn't believe in the Trinity. Did you know that the word Millennium is not in the Bible? The concept of the 1,000-year reign is. Which, 1,000 years means millennium. So, you can't believe in the millennium because the word millennium is not there? Did you know that the word Bible is not in the Bible? It's not, so should I not believe in the Bible? Again, if that is your logic, I have a problem with that. You want to know why abortion is wrong? Even if the word is not in the Bible, because abortion is murder and the Bible says that murder is wrong. And the murder of a person is wrong. The unborn child is a person and you shouldn't kill them, that is why we believe abortion is wrong because the concept is in the Scripture.

Now let me demonstrate this to you. Is it wrong to murder a person? Yes! Let me just give you some Scripture. **Genesis 9**; **Matthew 15**; **Matthew 19**; **Mark 10**; **Luke 18**; **John 8**; **Acts 3**; **Romans 1**; and **Romans 13.** Ok, murders are wrong. I think we would agree on that. But is an unborn child really a person? Yes, it is, let me give you a couple of examples. First of all, the Scripture tells us that the unborn possess personal attributes, which means they are a person. They may not be out of the womb yet, but they are still a person.

We see in **Psalm 51:5,** David says, "I was brought forth in iniquity and in sin my mother conceived me."

Luke 1:44: "Behold, when the sound of your breathing reached my ears, the baby leaped in my womb for joy."

Well if it is just a blob of tissue, how can it experience joy or be equated with sin, it's only something that people can refer to. The Scripture also refers to the unborn with pronouns. It's a real person because it is.

Jeremiah 1:5 "Before I formed you in the womb, I knew you." (*Not it.)* "And before you were born, I consecrated you and appointed you as a prophet to the nations."

Matthew 1: "When he had considered this behold an angel of the Lord appeared to him in a dream, saying Joseph son of David, do not be afraid to take Mary as your wife, for the child *(not it, not the blob of tissue, not an non-viable entity, or parasite.)* who was conceived in her is from the Holy Spirit. She will have a son and you shall call his name Jesus. For He shall save His people from their sins."

Notice the personal pronouns, because He's a real person. Also, Jesus was a baby at conception. We also see that where the angel tells Joseph that the child that was conceived is of the Holy Spirit. So, who determines the conception at that moment? God, the Holy Spirit, God, is the one. And it certainly indicates that Jesus was a person at the moment of conception. The Bible also calls the unborn, children. In Luke we see this again when Elizabeth heard Mary's greeting, the baby, not the blob of tissue, not the fetus, the baby leaped in her womb and Elizabeth was filled with the Holy Spirit. Also, did you know that the unborn in Scripture are protected by the same rights as the adults, including if you murder them?

Exodus 21:22,23 "If men struggle with each other and strike a woman with child so that she gives birth prematurely, yet there is no injury, he shall surely be fined as the woman's husband may demand of him and he shall pay as the judges decide. But if there is any further injury then you shall appoint as the penalty, life for life."

In the Old Testament if you injured or murdered a baby you got the death penalty. They weren't outside the womb yet. Just quoting the Scripture. They have the same rights as adults. Why? Because they are people. God also called them people before birth. He doesn't call them blobs of flesh; He calls them people.

Jeremiah 1:5 "Listen to me old islands and pay attention. You peoples from afar. The Lord called me from the womb and from the body of my mother he named me."

There are also the unborn known personally by God like any other person describing David.

Psalm 139 "My frame was not hidden from you God, when I was made in secret and skillfully wrought in the depths of the earth, my eyes have seen my unformed substance and in your book were all written the days that were ordained for me when as yet there was not one of them.

Also, in **Jeremiah 1:5** "Before I knew you in the womb, I knew you."

God was speaking of course. "Before you were born, I consecrated you and appointed you to a nation."

When you put that all together, they say that the Bible doesn't mention abortion. Excuse me, it's still wrong, it's a person. Here is what the Bible teaches. The unborn are persons because the unborn possesses personal attributes, they are described by personal pronouns, Jesus was a child at conception, by God and the Holy Spirit. The unborn are called children, they are protected with the same punishment as for an adult, they are called by God before birth, they are known personally by God just like any other person, therefore, abortion is wrong because it is murdering a person. Albeit a smaller person, but it is still a person. Murder is wrong, so this whole thing is wrong. Case closed. I have to share this one last thing. It almost made me sick! This was one of the comments that was on one of the videos that was still on YouTube before it got yanked off. This was supposed to be a guy that gives you the impression that he is an evangelist. Listen to what he has to say about one of our studies about the mass murder of children. And I quote:

"The Scripture says that a baby does not have a soul until they are born and receives God's gift of life. The life of the baby's is the mother's life. Abortion is not killing life. The Creator created a life with no life in it."

What? This is supposed to be a Christian Evangelist. I have to share this; it was shocking to me. Then he goes on to say...

"THE CHRISTIANS ARE LYING. When a husband and wife conceive, they make a lifeless body. The baby in the womb is not a human being. Abortion is not killing human babies; abortion is killing bodies with no soul in them."

Then he ends it with this....

Bless you,

Where do you even start on that? What Bible are you reading? Then this one guy surmised it.

"*We are allowed to take a life, in the Bible, as prescribed requirement of the law. Such as self-defense or war, a just war, not just any war, some wars are not just. Execution, things of that nature. Each of these deal within areas of the law. Self-defense is justified because an antagonist is breaking the law, i.e. Burglary, assault, robbery.*

"*We can use force to protect ourselves and our property or illegal hostilities towards another nation. Execution is taking a life of someone who has committed a crime or crimes worthy of execution. In each case the antagonist is dealt with for the crimes that they have wrought. But the baby in the womb has done no wrong.*

"*Yet, it's executed. It's executed but it has broken no law. What crime has been committed? What law have they broken in their existence? None, yet they are killed. I'm reminded of Nazi Germany. The Jews were guilty of just being Jews and according to the Nazi's, they were worthy of death. Likewise, these babies in the womb are guilty of just being babies in the womb and are, according to their parents, worthy of death.*

"*What laws did they break? What made them so unworthy of life? The answer is simple, it depends on the opinion of those in power, of those wielding the knife, and redefining what is life and those deciding who is worthy of life and who should die.*"

Folks, that is eugenics.

"*It's only an abortion if someone is executed but has not violated the law. This is fundamentally wrong, that's why abortion is wrong. Since when do we kill someone that has broken no law. Since when, do we kill someone whose only crime was being brought into existence via the copulation of his or her parents?*"

You're murdering the innocent. And yet somehow, it's supposed to be alright.

They have a couple different things they want to say as to why they need to have this right. They give us various reasons that it is their right to commit abortion. They say the life in the womb is not human because it is not fully developed. Alright, let's explore that. What constitutes fully developed? Is that one hour before birth? Is it an hour after birth? Is there a difference? Did you know that that is the game they play? Did you know that I have heard on record that there are some parents who still have their kids at home, and they are in their mid-twenties? And they haven't left? Are they fully developed? Maybe we should get rid of them. Where do you draw the line? Where is this mystical line of development when they become a real person? At what point does life suddenly develop value? If value is dependent on the choice of the mother, then how is it possible that the choice of the mother changes the nature of the life from valuable to valueless since there is no change in the condition of life in the womb. Just saying it's valuable doesn't determine that. If it's human in nature, how does it give anyone the right to kill it? If nature is something else, when does it change into a human? If it's a blob of tissue, when did it turn into a human? As we saw, it was human from conception. It's a lie.

Then they say if you aren't sure, is it something that you want to risk? "Well, I'm not really sure when it becomes a human." Again, it's human from conception but if you want to play their game, do you really want to risk killing a human if you don't really know when it becomes one? Is that something that you really want to flirt with? Again, that's a lie, because we know when it becomes a human.

The second thing they say is that the human tissue in the woman is the property of the one who produced it. You've heard that one, right? It's her body. But if what is growing in the womb is a person, and we can demonstrate that, biblically and scientifically, then they cannot be owned. They don't belong to you. Is the life in the womb property, like a cat or a dog that can be owned? When does the child stop being the property of the mother? If they say they own them because it is part of their body, does that ownership stop at birth? Or again, 1 year old, 2-year-old, 20-year-old? Is that the 25-year-old rule? If so, you better get out of the house. Oh, and by the way, it's animals that can be owned, not people. Unless you want to reintroduce slavery because that is a child in there. You don't own that person. Nobody owns people. Owning people is called slavery, are you for slavery? You can't have it both ways.

Another argument they have is that it is part of the woman and she has the right to do what she wants to do with her body. Really? Are you going to say that that baby, which is a person, is a part of your body? How many of you have seen a woman with 4 arms, 4 legs, 2 heads, and 4 eyes? Because if the baby is a part of you, then the baby has 2 legs, like you, which equals 4 legs in your body, two arms plus 2 arms, do you see where I'm going? That baby is not part of you. Her body is separate from the body growing in her. It's another body. The life growing in the womb can have a different blood type that the mother. It has separate brain waves. It is an independent life with its own DNA. Its nature is human, and it is a separate life from the mother. So no, it doesn't belong to you. It's in your body, but it's not part of your body. Oh, and by the way if it's just a part of your body, there should be absolutely no guilt with what you chose to do with your body. But when women choose to kill their children through abortion, then why is it that so many, if not all, feel guilty after the abortion? Right? Hey, I have a wart on me, I take it off and I feel so guilty. That's what you are saying. It's my body, I just got rid of another person, then why do you feel so guilty? Not just guilty, but so guilty that psychologically you can't handle it, and some end up killing themselves just because they got rid of them. No, it's not a part of your body. It's a different human inside your body.

Then of course, the next one is rape. With this one they take the most extreme example and try to make us believe that we should encompass all of murdering children. Did you know that not even 1%, 0.5% of abortions are done because of rape? But that's all you hear. You mean to tell me that you are going to make women be forced to give birth to that child? Did you notice the slip, child in there, you forgot to say fetus? Catch them on it when they do it. What did you just say? You said child. You admitted it is a child, didn't you? But they take the extreme example.

Let's take a look at the issue of rape. Rape is horrible. What is the punishment for rape in the Scripture? Death penalty. You bring that back and guess what is going to happen to that behavior. It's going to go down. It is horrible, but here's the question. Why should the child in the womb pay for the sins of the other person? Again, what crime did it commit? The baby is innocent of the offense and its life need not be taken away because of the act of another person. Oh, and remember it's all about choice. I have a choice to do that. But where is the baby's choice in all this? And if you're all about choice, let's be fair about it. You have three people involved in a rape, which is horrible, I'm not condoning rape, of course not, but it happens and sometimes a baby is the result. But you've got three people, and you want to be fair. Is it all about choice? You have three people, you give each one a dice to roll, have the doctor roll for the baby since the baby is in the womb, roll the dice and whoever gets the lowest number, that's the one that dies. I mean if it's all about choice and you're trying to be fair, why is it that the one that committed no crime is the one that has to die?

By the way, guess what? You can put the baby up for adoption. If you can't handle thinking about that child, maybe it does remind you of the rapist, then put it up for adoption. There's always a way, even in the existence and horrible occurrence of rape, that you still don't need to murder the child. But listen to this. The percentage of infants given up for adoption in the United States declined from 9% born before 1973 to .5% in 2014 because so many are being murdered. As a result, the number of U.S. infant adoptions dropped. About 2.6 million Americans are seeking to adopt children right now but they can't get their hands on them because they are being killed right and left. Rape victims are 4 times more likely to die in the next year after an abortion, with a higher rate of suicide, drug overdose, murder, etc. As someone who really cares about rape victims, I want to protect them not only from the rapist, I also want to protect them from the murderous effects of abortion. A baby is not the worst thing that could happen to a rape victim but statistically, rape and abortion is. So again, which one do you choose?

Another one that is restricting a woman's right to choose or denying her rights, but nobody has the right to murder a child. Did you know that 50% of unborn children are girls? The unborn female has a body that is separate from that of her mother. She has her own unique DNA; her genetic code directs the development and growth of her own body from the moment of conception. Therefore, an abortion takes away the rights of a woman. It's all about the rights of a woman but here you are taking away the rights of a woman. It takes away her rights, the baby in the womb, to control her own body. It takes away her right to choose anything in the future. It takes away a right more fundamental than the right to choose, i.e. the right to not be killed. Where's the right to those girls if you're for women's rights?

Then they say, we have to make abortion legal because women will die if we have unsafe abortions. And it will be really unsafe if we don't legalize it. Really? Let's explore that. The argument begs the question, is it okay for society to sanction child murder just because someone might do it anyway? Let's press that logic. Should we legalize rape so that the government can make it safer and cleaner? Should we legalize underground sex slave trade, and regulate it so we can make it safer and cleaner for the people because they are going to do it anyway? That was a myth concocted by the abortion industry. Dr. Bernard Nathanson, co-founder of the national abortion rights action league, admitted that he and other abortion industry leaders invented the figures that thousands of women are going to die annually from unsafe abortions. They did this in order to get public sympathy to make abortion legal.

Another one, they say, well there are just too many people in the world. Where do you start with that one? We already saw that over population is a myth, it's a lie. If you think this world is overpopulated, get in a plane, travel anywhere, look out the window. They always show downtown China, Shanghai, New York city, the city of Los Angeles, but if you look out the window there is plenty of room on the earth. It's a lie. And if you are so concerned about the earth being populated (tongue in cheek) then why are you advocating killing somebody else? Why don't you volunteer? Again, tongue in cheek, I'm not advocating that. I'm just saying follow your own logic. Where this is leading, of course, is euthanasia. They want to determine who lives and who doesn't. They say if abortion is legal it should be okay. Did you know that 150 years ago slavery was legal? So, it must be okay. No, just because something is legal doesn't mean it's okay. Did you know that in the books in Germany, they said the Jewish people were not a people? That was on the legal books. So, go get 'em, kill 'em. Does that make it right? Well, that's what is being done here.

Then they throw this one out there. You Christians are violating the Bible because the Bible says that Christians should submit to the government and the government says abortion is legal, so you need to submit. They say it's abuse of Romans 13 that talks about being subject to the rules over you but there is always that biblical caveat, unless that government asks you to do something contrary to the Scripture, i.e. God's will. Abortion is murder and we already demonstrated murder is against God's will. So, society says I need to go out there and murder people, including children in the womb, I am against that. I have the ability from God to say, NO! In fact, the Bible also says in Acts 5, that we are to obey God rather than men. *"Peter and the other apostles replied, we must obey God, rather than men."* Right? God always supersedes all of that. If you are so hooked on obeying the government, listen to this, speaking of the need to obey. Did you know that unborn babies right now are considered human beings by the U.S. Government? Why don't we ever see this one on the news? The Federal Unborn Victims of Violence Act which was enacted to protect unborn children from assault and murder states that under law, anybody intentionally killing or attempting to kill an unborn child should be punished for intentionally killing or attempting to kill an unborn human being. It also states that an unborn child is a member of the species of homo sapiens and at least 38 states have passed a similar fetal homicide law. That's on the books. So, if you're so big on that you have to obey the government, why aren't you obeying that law? And how come that law is never being brought up?

Let me give you two more. The Hippocratic Oath. You are supposed to be a medical doctor. One section of the Hippocratic Oath reads *"I will not give a woman a device inserted into the vaginal canal to cause an abortion."* That is a direct quote. Also, it says, *"It forbids doctors from performing abortions, above all I must not play God."* So, you are not only violating the laws of the government that you are so concerned about, but if you are in the medical industry, you are violating the Hippocratic Oath. Even our founding fathers said you are violating the unalienable right. The Declaration of Independence states that all men are created equal, they are endowed by their creator with certain unalienable rights, these are life, liberty, and the pursuit of happiness. Abortion takes away from the unborn the unalienable right that the founding fathers intended for all human beings. So, if you're so hung up on it, that we have to obey the law, you are violating it yourself in major ways. Now here's what's mind-blowing. How many hours, how many days, how many years do we sit here and talk about abortion, it's wrong, abortion, it's wrong, abortion, and I'm not saying that we shouldn't, but do you realize the whole time we were talking about it, the abortion counter is still going on? In the time that you have been reading this chapter, if you go online and check, they are killing a baby per second all over the world. It's been going on all day, and it will keep going on all night, so when you check it again in the morning you can see how many have died.

I want to end this chapter with this one, because this is the issue. The greatest thing we could do to give a defense is that we need to stand up for God's truth that condemns this murderous practice. We need to do it not only for the person, but because sin hurts, sin harms and destroys, but it kills the child. We do it in defense of the baby as well. You might be witnessing to someone that has already done the deed and at that point, that is where you need to give a loving response. You don't deny it, you don't act like it didn't happen, you don't try to soften it, but the greatest deed you can do at that point is to encourage them to confess it to God, and be forgiven so that they can finally begin the process of healing. Like these ladies.

"After my sixth abortion I felt like I was going crazy and literally began to bang my head against the wall. Within a few short months I found myself in a church and I heard the pastor start talking about the Scripture, 'I haven't given you a spirit of fear, but a spirit of love, a spirit of power, a spirit of sound mind' and he also started to say that I think there is somebody here today that has been thinking about committing suicide. About taking your life, and I want you to come forward and let me pray for you. And I moved forward that day because I was desperate to get off of that Merry-go-round of abortion.

I had to confess out loud that I was responsible for the deaths of two of my children through abortion. It was the hardest thing I ever did in my whole life to speak it out loud, but when I did the healing began. The grieving began.

Once I became a Christian, God began opening my eyes to the truth about abortion. He began over the years, slowly exposing the reality of abortion to me and I finally realized that it wasn't a blob of tissue that was inside of me. That abortion took the life of my child and I began to realize that I was responsible for killing four of my own children.

I can remember taking my hands and placing them on the bed and crying out to God and asking him, 'Lord, help me, forgive me, for what I've done and I started to just open my Bible, because at that time there were no abortion recovery Bible studies and He had me look at one Scripture and it was ***I John 1:9*** *'If we confess our sins, I am faithful to forgive you of every sin and to cleanse you of all unrighteousness.' I began crying out to Him for that forgiveness. I can remember that day that I did, that I could feel a release in my heart from all of the pain that had been there from all the abortions.*

Two weeks later after I found out I was pregnant, I actually accepted Jesus Christ as my savior at a Crisis Pregnancy Center.

My mom had come to know the Lord and she called me one day. During the conversation on the phone she started talking to me of the love of Jesus Christ and the hope in Him. And she started telling me how much she loved me, and how much she cared for me, and no matter what I could have done, that God would still love me. So, I came home that night to my parents' house and went to a conference with them and I received the Lord Jesus as my savior. And my life changed.

It was my parents that sat me down after a while and said they thought that there was something very emotional going on and that is why you are so ill, and you seem so sad and at that moment something in me snapped. I began to weep uncontrollably. I couldn't speak and it was my mother that turned to me and said, Kelly, did you have an abortion? It took me a little bit to confess, that yes, I had and then we were able to pray.

At this retreat, the first testimony I heard was this girl who had two abortions and how God healed her and forgave her. That weekend I gave my life to the Lord and I was forgiven for having my abortion.

"My husband and I were invited to a fund-raising banquet at a local Crisis Pregnancy Center and I felt so out of place until the next speaker came up and it was a woman talking about her abortion and the healing she received. I just wanted what this woman was talking about. Freedom in Jesus, for once and for all to lay that sin at the feet of Jesus, receive healing and go on to help other women."

Not deny it, not pacify it, not hide it, not justify it, just confess it to Jesus Christ. I like what she said, and then go tell other women who had also made that mistake to do the same. So, they can be set free. That is how we respond. In the next two chapters we'll look at the future of abortion. Where is all this headed? As we saw a couple chapters back, they are already talking about killing babies after birth, but it is even beyond that. They are thinking about murdering children with Down Syndrome. At this rate they are also coupling it with assisted suicide and euthanasia. If you're going to kill a child, as they would say is a nuisance and a financial obligation, then what about those old people? I tell you that is exactly where it is headed, and we need to get equipped on that as well.

Chapter Seven

The Future of Abortion Part 1

Where we are headed with this is not good. We are already murdering 10's of millions of children, and that is bad. You are literally killing your future. As we saw before, if we don't speak up now it is going to get even worse. If you think it is bad with them killing 10's of millions in the womb, I'm telling you, they are already going outside the womb and they are not going to stop there. They are going to go to the other end of the spectrum, they are going to start knocking off adults. We will get to that as well. But this is the kind of brutal, wicked, behavior that the Bible said would appear on the world scene when you are living in the last days.

2 Timothy 3:1-5 *"But mark this: There will be terrible times in the last days. People will be lovers of themselves...*

What is the number one verse in our society today? Love yourself. Self-respect. Self-esteem. The Bible says if you want some loving, you love God first. Love your neighbor, that's down the list. You want to love somebody; you esteem others above yourself. You want some respect; you need to give the Savior respect for all he has done for you. You want to be a disciple of Jesus Christ; the first thing you must do is deny yourself, pick up your cross and follow Him, so as to make it a habit of life. Our world is infatuated with selfism, which is the number one law of satanism, do what you will. That is the celebrated version today, as we saw with abortion, murdering children and what is the big reason for people killing their children? Self, whether it is for greed or a selfish decision. I don't want to deal with this, I don't have time, I, I, I, I, same thing.

...lovers of money...

That certainly goes along with the abortion movement.

...boastful, proud...

Wait until you see the abortion movement and their behavior in just a bit.

...abusive, disobedient to their parents, ungrateful, unholy, without love, unforgiving, slanderous, without self-control, brutal, not lovers of the good, treacherous, rash, conceited, lovers of pleasure rather than lovers of God...

You know, I can't come to church services, there's a game on, I can't come to Wednesday night service, there is a great show on, and the DVR broke, no actually it didn't break I just want to stay home and watch it, and what's that? Lovers of pleasure rather than lovers of God.

...having a form of godliness...

They say they are spiritual; they say they are Christians; they say they love God.

...but denying its power...

Hang out with these people because we are all supposed to be one in this giant ecumenical movement, as we display our love for one another.

...Have nothing to do with them"

So again, the Bible is very clear on this. These are some clear-cut signs of society that will appear in the world when you are living in the last days, in that generation, like it or not. But basically, in a nutshell, what you are seeing is the world is going to be so filled with absolute unadulterated wickedness non-stop, everything you can think of. Which by the way is a repeat of the prophecy that Jesus said, "As it was in the days of Noah, so shall it be with the coming of the Son of Man." Before Jesus comes back you are going to see a repeat of Noah's day. And one of the things, in the Genesis account, in Noah's day, was society was so wicked they just thought wickedness continually, the Scripture said. And it grieved the heart of God. And Paul says it's going to be repeated again in the last days. He said, 'They are going to be selfish, greedy and boastful, prideful, abusive, disobedient, ungrateful, unholy, unloving, unforgiving, slanderous, out of control, conceited, brutal, and evil,' every single one, name one that's not going on today. It's not 50-50, we have a half more to go. Or 2/3, well we have another 1/3 to go, we aren't there yet. It's 100%, going on in our world right now. And dare I say even in the church, in what you call church-world.

This is a sign we are in the last days, and we are that generation, and I want to focus on that word brutal. Brutal is the Greek word, anemeros, which means to not be tame, to be savage, to be fierce. You look at that and wonder of wonders, isn't that also going on in our world today? How people are treating each other? If I want a pair of sneakers and you have them and I don't, I will kill you to get them. That is savage, fierce, that is brutal. That is anemeros. When you take a child in the womb and you literally pull its limbs off piece by piece that is anemeros, brutal. That is not just nuts, that is savage. What kind of people do that? But that is what Paul said is going to be the scene. You're going to act like a bunch of savages. And I think that certainly fits with this whole thing of abortion, amongst other things, that we are seeing in our society as well. How flippant people are to kill one another, especially children, limb by limb. But what I want to do is to let you know about the future. Because if this savage behavior doesn't stop, it's going to get even worse. You think it's bad now, you ain't seen nothing yet! Because they will not, and they are not going to stop in the womb. We are going to see they are already going outside the womb, they are going to the other end of the spectrum and they are going to start knocking off people until they create their perfect society.

Let me give you a breakdown. How are they going to create that last days society, brutally wicked, with what we are seeing now? Well, the first way, is you brutally, savagely, murder children in the womb. This is sort of a recap of where we have been so far, but I want you to see how they are not stopping with this wicked brutal behavior of murdering children in the womb. It's going to go outside and keep on going. This is what you do first. To show you how brutal and how savage that really is, right now in our country, it is legal to kill these babies in all 50 states. Again, don't use their terminology and don't hide behind the

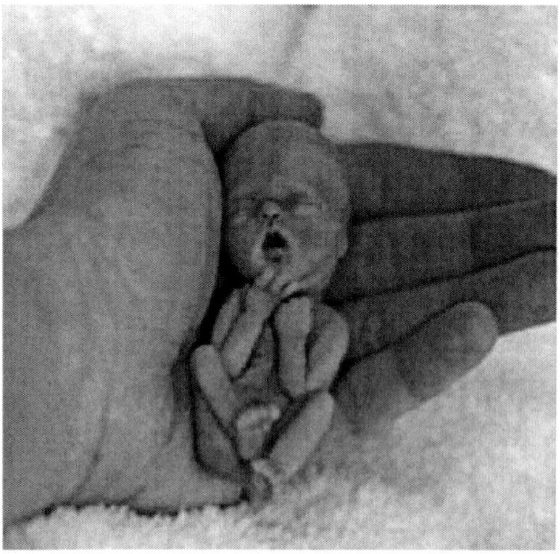

verbiage, but when you expose it for what it is, this is what's going on. This is the brutal, savage, wicked behavior in our country today. This is a baby at 12 weeks, and in all 50 states they are killing them, by the millions. It's smaller, but it is still a baby. I'm smaller than a lot of people, and that's right, I'm somebody's baby. In fact, how many can verify this scientific proof. Did you realize that it has been scientifically proven that if your parents didn't have any children, you won't either? That is probably going to be the only joke in this chapter, because this is a very serious topic. But seriously, that is brutal, that's wicked. All 50 states are murdering children like that, and it's legal. But as we saw before, just because it is legal doesn't make it right. This is also why they are saying the most dangerous place in the world is in the womb. It is! Especially if you are an impoverished person. Especially if you are in a minority group, because that is what eugenics, Margaret Sanger, wants to do, to get rid of the non-Caucasians. You talk about racist! Everybody is talking about racism in our country! Let's start talking about Planned Parenthood! But the most dangerous place in the United States, is in the womb. And dare I say, even around the world. Oh, and by the way, you want to talk about brutal, insane, wicked behavior? I have to share this. Why would a bacterium be considered life on Mars, and we know that scientifically, but you refuse to believe a heartbeat is considered to be life on earth? Does anybody see how brutal that is, and how ridiculous that is? Which by the way, has led to this truth. You can see the headline from LifeNews.com which was from December, just a couple of months ago. Abortion is the leading cause of death worldwide, killing 42 million people in one year. Abortion is the leading cause of

death. How many times do you hear it on the news?

LifeNews.com

Abortion Was the Leading Cause of Death Worldwide in 2018, Killing 42 Million People

It's all over the place, hey, we have a cure for cancer. Tonight, there was a show on lung cancer. I'm glad they are talking about it. They talk about cancer, suicide, alcoholism, and all these diseases or other crisis' but we had 42 million children die just last year. It's the number one cause of death on our planet and nobody wants to talk about it. Then if they do talk about it, "Don't you tell me I can't do that." Now that is a brutal society. That is anemeros! Now let me give you a little bit more on those statistics. This is from the same article from LifeNews.com.

LifeNews.com reports: *"More human beings died in abortions than any other case of death in 2018, a new report indicates. The abortion numbers compared to other causes of death are far out in advance, it outweighs cancer, HIV, AIDS, traffic accidents, suicide, and found that abortions far outnumber every single* *one of them. In fact, that number does not include unborn babies or abortion deaths. Unborn babies are not recognized as human beings by society, even though biologically they are uniquely living beings at the moment of conception."*

So, it may be even bigger than that. But that's what's going on. And this is their words, from that same article, "*They die brutal, violent deaths in abortion.*" That is exactly what Paul said would come on the scene when you are living in the last days. Now, the reason why it is escalating is because once again unfortunately, the church, which is supposed to be the light in the darkness, and by the way, the problem, as we have seen before, it's not with the darkness per say. I'm not condoning darkness, but the problem isn't so much the darkness as it is the light refusing to shine. You want to get rid of the darkness? If you go into a dark room and you want to get rid of the darkness, what do you do? You flip on the light. What happens to the darkness? Bang, it's gone! The problem is the church, the ones who know better, who have the light of God's truth, who can steer people out of this dark path and illuminate the way, we're not doing anything about it. So that's another thing we need to consider. Another reason why it is increasing, is because it is being encouraged. This brutal, anemeros behavior, and part of it is from the abortion movement themselves. These people are getting brutal. It's sick, it's savage, they are actually celebrating murdering their children. Here's just one example of that. There is a new movement out there, it's called '#shout your abortion.' It's sick, now again, translate it for what it is. Don't use their words, let's translate it, '#shout murdering your child.' It's not just sick, it's savage! That is what savages do. Let's celebrate killing people. That's a sign you're living in the last days that Paul talked about. Just shout your abortion on the internet. Let me give you a couple more pictures.

They are making T-shirts. She is walking around the neighborhood, she is walking around the world, doing what? Shouting the murdering of her child. Because that is what it is. Right? Then, of course, she does not regret the murdering of her child in public. That is the savage, savage world that we live in. It's being encouraged. Murder is being encouraged. Who would have thought, but that is a sign that we are living in the last days that the Scripture talks about. Also, someone that has jumped on the bandwagon is Oprah Winfrey. The biggest New Age priestess on the planet.

Oprah Winfrey had this 'Shout your abortion' or murder your child in her magazine. That's unfortunate, because not only is she the biggest New Ager on the planet, if you doubt that, get our study on New Age and the Last Days Deception. We have a chapter called Oprah Winfrey, but unfortunately she has 10's of millions of people that follow her from around the world and what is her magazine promoting? Don't feel guilty, be brutal, join the movement, shout killing your child. That is the society that we are living in today. To go even further, they have these pendants that they are offering, an abortion pendant, a hanger, isn't that sick?

Again, as we saw before, the figures they use to draw sympathy, to get people to go past the Roe vs Wade, doctors admitted that they jacked up the numbers, it's all inflated. Supposedly thousands of women are dying because of these unhealthy practices so we have to make the practices healthy. We have people being wrongfully raped, so do we make industry standards for those people to go and rape people safely? That's ridiculous, but that was the justification. Oh, and they are mocking you and I, they are mocking our Lord Jesus Christ with aborted Jesus Christ dolls.

What a brutal, sick society. Man, God is watching all this, folks! This is getting wicked in our world today, in the last days. In New York you can now murder your child, and it will be drawn out with pictures, because you can say, "It's 12 weeks old." Well we just saw a picture of a 12-week-old baby. That's a baby. Well, it's only in the first trimester, second trimester, third trimester, and they hide behind that. In New York state they can murder every one of these children. Let's take a look.

Live Action News: *"In New York, it's now legal to abort babies at this age, born at 22 weeks.*

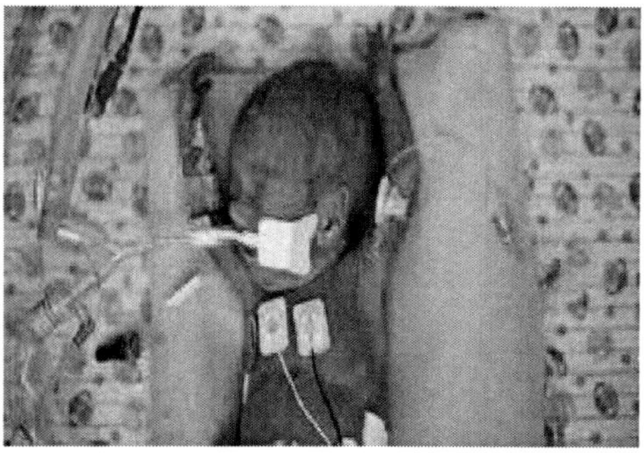

In New York, it's now legal to abort babies at 24 weeks. (see below)

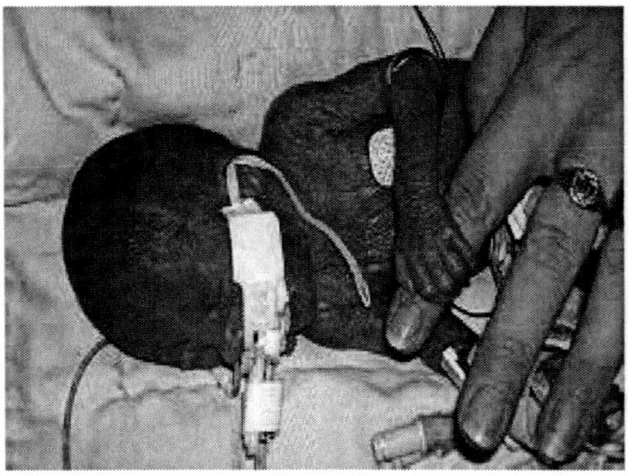

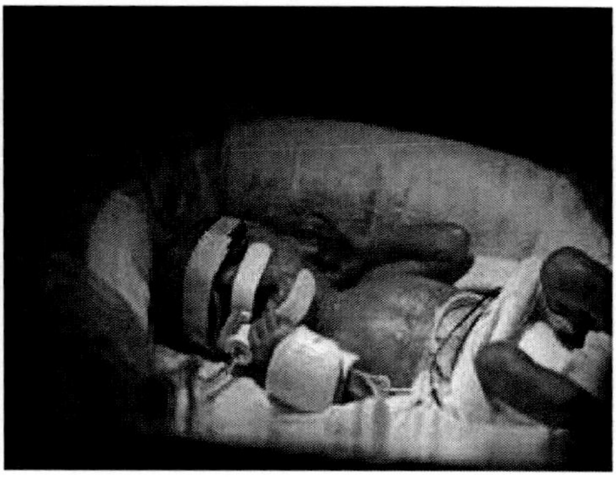

In New York, it's now legal to abort babies at this age, born at 30 weeks (see below)

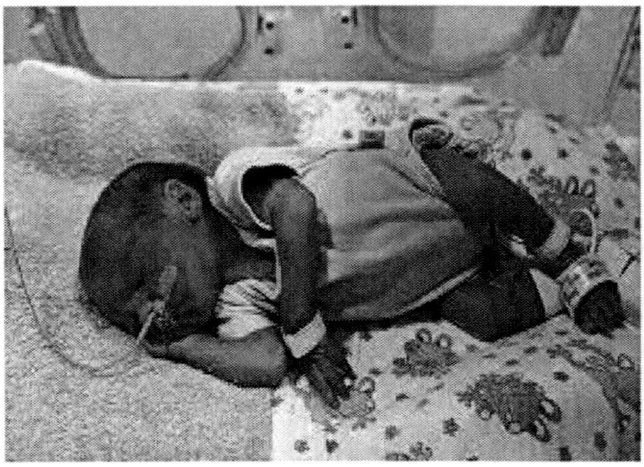

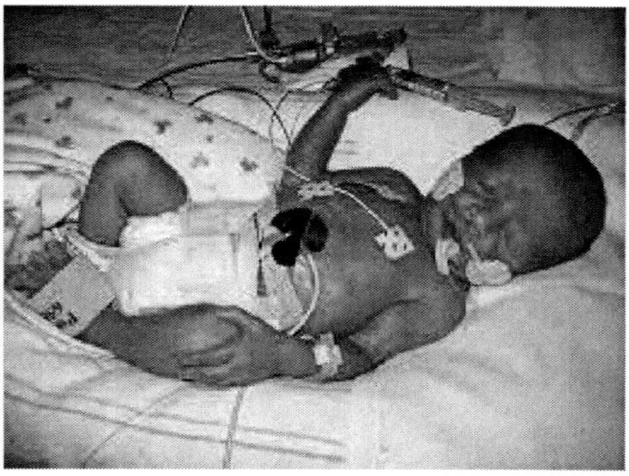

Those are children. Don't hide behind your weeks, your gestation period. They are murdering children, and that is brutal! That is savagery, that's anemeros. That's our world today. And they are celebrating it. You wonder why the wrath of God is coming for 7 years, non-stop? That last one was 30 weeks. We also saw in New York; they are murdering them all the way up to birth. So, it's even older than that. That is what they are doing. That's bad! But Praise God, there is a little bit of a crack in the dam, so to speak, of this brutal, savage behavior, this mass murder of children. There are some states that are starting to turn around and we need to be speaking up. Let me give you a couple examples. One from Kentucky and one from Georgia. This was just a few weeks ago.

"The Kentucky Legislature just passed two bills on abortion this week and unless the court blocks the proceeding, abortion will be officially banned in the state."

One bill prohibits abortions 6 weeks into pregnancy, before most women even know that they are pregnant. The other that was passed bans a woman seeking it because of a fetal diagnosis i.e. a baby diagnosis. What is that all about? To see if it has any defects. Because we know it's a baby, but if it is a defective baby, then let's go ahead and kill it. I'm telling you, that is where it is all headed, and it's already being done. The ACLU is challenging both laws. Now if there are those of you that don't understand the acronym it's 'The American Communist Lawyers Union', actually, it's Civil, but I call it Communist. Now why are states all of a sudden starting to turn around? Because we as a Christian community are being emboldened by the Trump Administration. This President stands on life. So other states are considering doing so as well, including Ohio, Tennessee, Texas, Missouri, Florida, Alabama and Georgia.

Speaking of Georgia, listen to this. Georgia is the latest state to pass a Fetal Heartbeat Bill as part of a growing trend. So, there is a light on the horizon. This is not a time to sit back on our haunches and go back to sleep. We need to speak up and capitalize on the crack in the dam. Listen to this though. The Bill which narrowly passed in the Republican controlled legislation, who controlled? I'm going to be blunt again. The Democrat Party has turned into the Death Party and I don't care who it is, Democrat or Republican, I hear there are Republicans who support abortion i.e. murdering children. You shouldn't support them either. By and large, 100% it seems, in the Democrat Party, there is no option but death. And if you can be a Christian with good conscience and vote for any one of those people, I have a problem with that, and you should too.

"In the Republican controlled legislature, on Friday, Trump is expected to sign a law, by Bryan Kemp, a Republican. The measure generally prohibits the procedure if the doctors can discern a baby's heartbeat, a milestone that happens around 6 weeks before some women even know they are pregnant."

So, again, we are seeing some signs, seeing bills in these states and they are doing it on purpose because they know that it will lead to the Supreme Court and then we can get rid of this Roe vs Wade thing. Guess who's flipping out on this? You would think, who would flip out on this? We know that this is a child. Now we are talking about a 'Heartbeat Bill' that we can detect an actual heartbeat. You know it's a human, who could be against that? Hollywood and the Democrats are going nuts over what these states are doing. Saving children! Let me give you a couple of examples.

In an article from April 1st, 2019. *"Actors who consider the boycott of Georgia after state passes 'Heartbeat Bill Abortion Bill."*

Now remember these are the same people that said they were going to leave the country if Trump got elected, and they are still here.

"Hollywood's elite are joining together to call on the Republican Governor Bryan Kemp to veto Georgia's new anti-abortion 'Heartbeat Bill.' Responding to the bill, actress Alyssa Milano started a petition, and she and others said they would not be able to work in Georgia in good conscience."

What kind of conscience do you have and how can you call it good when you are upset when it is protecting children and you want them to continue being murdered? What kind of a conscience is that? The Bible has a word for that, it's called a seared conscience.

"About 50 Hollywood actors, including Alyssa Milano, Amy Schumer, and Ben Stiller, wrote an open letter, threatening to pull business out of the state." "We want to continue to support the wonderful people and businesses in the communities we have come to love in the Peach State, but we will not do so silently and we will do everything in our power to move our industry to a safer state for women if this becomes law."

Do you see the sick, brutal irony there? "I can't believe they are wanting to ban murdering children that we know are children because we are detecting heartbeats." They have to find a safer place. What a seared conscience. How do you justify that? The little 'g', the god satan, blinds the minds of those who do not believe. They don't even see it. They can't see what they are doing. I'm not justifying it or making it easy, they are responsible for it, talk about a spiritual battle. Let me just call out a couple other names. I have this list of 50, but I don't recognize some of them because I don't really care about Hollywood.

Christina Applegate, Alec Baldwin, Don Cheadle, Mia Farrow, Rosie O'Donnell, Sean Penn, Michael Sheen, and a whole bunch more. *'We are going to leave the state of Georgia if you protect children'.* Now that's not just ridiculous, that is brutal! That is savage! That is what savage people do. But that is what is happening in our world today. It is the last days society being created.

But, not just the Hollywood liberals, but again so are the Democrats, which once again I call the Death Party. And again, how can you vote for these people? I have no clue and I hope you don't. I hope you vote, but you don't vote Democrat. I'm just going to be blunt; they have turned into the Death Party. I don't work for the Republicans. I don't work for any of those political people. I'm just saying that statistically, 100%, they always seem to be for killing children now. Then I came across this. I thought I was done with my notes, but this is hot off the press. This was Monday night. I was watching Tucker Carlson on Fox News and he just happened to have this little blip about Democrat Stacy Abrams. Remember her? She was running in Georgia, lost and she is still throwing a fit to this day. He had a clip of why she is against this 'Heartbeat Bill' that was passed to protect children in Georgia. This is her reason as to why and she calls the Bill an abomination.

Tucker Carlson: "*The State Legislature in the state of Georgia passed HB481 the 'Heartbeat Bill' the law which awaits the signature of the Georgia Governor. It is pretty straight forward with the usual exceptions for rape, incest and the life of the mother. Physicians in Georgia would be sanctioned for performing abortions after a child's heartbeat can be detected. The left hates the bill of course, it's not specifically designed to protect illegal aliens, for example, and famous people in California have promised to boycott Georgia if HB481 becomes law. What is interesting though is what the abortion lobby hasn't said about it. Nobody is saying that the bill won't save lives. It's pretty hard to argue that a child whose heart is beating isn't a living human being, instead, here is the argument they are using against it. Listen as the former Georgia legislator, Stacy Abrams, explains on MSNBC over the weekend.*"

Stacy Abrams: "*We have to be a state that not only has to be friendly to business, but you have to be friendly to the women who work in these businesses. You should not have to worry about your ability to control your bodily economy because the Governor has pushed such an abdominal evil bill that is so restricted. It's not only bad for our economy and humanity but it is bad for business.*"

Tucker Carlson: *"It's bad for business. So according to Stacy Abrams who went to Yale Law School, protecting the life of a child, whose heart is beating is evil because, as she just said, it is bad for business."*

If only I could find the right word to describe that mentality, it rhymes with brutal, it's savage. Did you see her words? It was an abomination, it's bad for business, that is a savage, savage, sick, society! I'll say it again; the Democrat party has become the Death Party.

Now that's just step one. They are going to create this society that is wicked and evil, and you wonder why the wrath of God is coming for 7 years, non-stop? That is just the first step to create an anemeros society. That is just children inside the womb. Now, unfortunately, you need to take it even further. Now you need to start killing children outside the womb. That is what we already saw is in the conversation with the Democrat Governor and his state representative saying it's okay and that's a discussion you should be able to have after the baby has been born, should you kill it then? Let's recap that just a little bit.

EWTN News Nightly: *"President Trump denounces a bill in Virginia that would have made abortion legal up to the moment a woman is giving birth. As outrage over the measure spreads out across the country, he tells the Daily Caller he thinks the Delegate Kathy Trans' proposal is terrible and reaffirms his rejection of late term abortions. Virginia Delegate Kathy Tran pitched her bill that shocked the American's earlier this week.*

Todd Gilbert: *"The woman is about to give birth, she is showing physical signs that she is about to give birth, would that be a point in which she could request an abortion if she was so certified? She's dilating."*

Kathy Tran: *"Mr. Chairman that would be a, you know, a decision that the doctor, the physician, and the woman would...."*

Todd Gilbert: *"I understand that. I'm asking if your bill allows that."*

Kathy Tran*:* *"My bill would allow that. Yes."*

EWTN News*:* *"Virginia house Majority Leader Todd Gilbert is heard questioning the Democrat."*

Todd Gilbert: *"She's the mother of four. To put it in terms, the darkest possible terms for her, was to make her own up to what her bill actually said. It may have been even unsettling for her."*

EWTN: *"And unsettling for President Trump. He tells the Daily Caller it's terrible. Then he brings up this line from the 2016 debates."*

President Trump: *"If you go with what Hillary is saying, in the ninth month you can take the baby and rip it out of the womb of the mother just prior to the birth of the baby."*

EWTN News: *"Governor Ralph Northam of Virginia is also facing backlash after his support for the bill."*

Ralph Northam: *"The infant would be delivered, the infant would be kept comfortable, the infant would be resuscitated if that is what the mother and the family desired, and then the discussion would ensue between the physician and the mother."*

Todd Gilbert: *"We found out that our Governor is willing, basically, to embrace the notion that if a child is born alive you actually just keep the child comfortable while you discuss how or whether to allow it to die."*

Die, when? Now the baby is outside the womb, it's completely outside the womb, the baby is on the table being kept comfortable as they have a discussion. Do they kill it, or do they not kill it? This is going on right now in our country. Evil is abounding and we need to speak up. But it's not going to stop. This is what happens. What does the Bible say? A little bit of yeast leavens the lump, it begins to spread, we have rolled over and played dead to our own detriment in disobedience to God. As the light in this dark world, that is doing this dark behavior, and we thought it would actually stop there. No, it's going outside the womb now. To their credit, that is a sick, brutal, savage, discussion, but it did spark an outrage. I don't think it got as big as it could have been in our country, remember what we saw before, just after a couple days after this started to broadcast, what did they bring out in the news 24/7 to distract you from what he just said? The black face issue. Oh, he had a yearbook with a black face. I'm not supporting racism whatsoever, but that was the smoke screen to get you off of what he just said because what he is promoting is infanticide. It's wrong to kill children any time, because they are babies at conception. But it did stir everyone's attention up, even with the trickery. In Congress, it did stir up some behavior. One of the Congressmen, Ben Sasse, produced a Bill, saying we are not just talking inside the womb but now we are in the dangerous conversation of outside the womb. We are going to put in a Bill that we can never cross that line. Never! It is an actual Bill. Just recently, in light of this guy's comments, the Democrat from Virginia and the Democrat Representative, Kathy Tran, can you believe that Bill did not pass?

Ben Sasse: "*This place fancies itself the world's greatest deliberative body, but we would be deceiving ourselves if we ignored the biggest debate that is happening in America over the last 36 hours. A public elected official, a Governor of one of the 50 states has been defending a practice that is morally repugnant. The Governor of Virginia has been defending a practice that is repugnant to civilized people across the entire world.*

"Here is just one of the ugly nuggets from Ralph Northam, the Governor of Virginia, 'If the mother is in labor, the infant would be delivered, the infant would be kept comfortable, the infant would be resuscitated, if the mother and the family so desired, and then a discussion would ensue between the physician and the mother.' Let's be really clear about what we are talking about here.

"We are talking about a fourth trimester abortion. Or, what anyone in the normal world calls infanticide. That's what we are talking about. The Governor of Virginia has been defending this all day yesterday and again today. Going out and trying to equivocate and qualify and then double down and again say he wants to defend his practice, which is infanticide. Let's be clear about what we are talking about.

"We are talking about killing a baby that's been born. We're not talking about euphemism, we're not talking about a clump of cells, we're talking about a little baby girl whose been born and is on a table in a hospital or a medical facility and then a decision or a debate would be had about whether or not you can kill that little baby. We are talking about the most vulnerable among us and we have a public official in America out there again and again supporting the practice. This is infanticide we are talking about.

"This should be so far beyond any political consideration. We are talking about a little baby, a baby with dignity, an image bearer, we are talking about a tiny life that has done nothing wrong to warrant being left to die, cold and alone on a

table. Everyone in this Senate ought to be able to say unequivocally that killing that little baby is wrong.

"This doesn't take any political courage. And if you can't say that, if there is a member of this body that can't say that, there may be lots of work you can do in the world, but you shouldn't be here. You should get the heck out of any kind of public life where you pretend to care about the most vulnerable among us. There should be no politics here where there are right verses left, Republican verses Democrat, this is the most basic thing you could be talking about. We are talking about a little baby born alive and we have a public official in America defending the idea, 'Oh you can have a debate about killing her.'"

FOX News: *"Just a short time ago on Capitol Hill, there was a defeat for a pro-life bill on the Senate floor. This bill was very specific, it would only protect infants who survived abortions at the end of the term by requiring health care officials to treat them with the same degree and skill as they would any other baby. But it was short the 60 votes needed to advance."*

How does that happen? Who in their right minds would vote against that? And then the status of our country. There are not enough people with common sense to realize we are talking about a child. It's wrong to murder children any time. From conception forward, it's wrong to murder. Period! We're outside of the womb now, on the table, and the Bill didn't pass. You know what that is? That is a brutal, savage society. By the way, guess who made sure it didn't pass? The Democrats, the Death Party. They worked together and they made sure that bill wasn't going to pass. There is no question it is a child. They know it's a child, they admit it is a child, it's a child on the table, it's a child being made comfortable, and the Democrats said, NOPE! We're going to make sure this thing tanks. To protect the life of that child, I will say it again, I'll be blunt, if you vote for any Democrat, shame on you as a Christian. The Democrat Party is rallying around this issue and made their brutal cry, 'We stand for the Murder of Children!' How you can throw your hat in the ring with those people as a Christian? You will be accountable for that!

Speaking of Democrats, that Governor, Ralph Northam, talk about a sick, brutal, twisted irony, he just passed a bill to make animal cruelty a felony. So, the exact same guy who supported killing children outside the womb makes his big debut by passing this bill. Do you see the sick, twisted, brutal, irony there? Here's what the article says:

"Earlier this year Governor Northam came under massive national criticism for appearing on a radio show supporting infanticide. He says, 'I don't have any regrets', and while protecting newborn babies who survived abortion attempts, and apparently too much for Northam to support, a law against animal cruelty isn't. Today, signed a new bill into law that would make animal cruelty a felony. Current law requires the animal to die before anyone could face felony charges, but under Northam's new bill, animal abusers will be found guilty of a felony. It increases the penalty for cruelty, or unnecessary beating or maiming, or mutilating or killing a dog or a cat to a felony charge."

I'm for that, but what is the irony of it? Here is a guy that says that you can have a child on a table, that we should have the right to decide whether to kill it or not, but let's protect a dog or a cat with a felony. But they say, "*The crime matches the penalty.*" Not whether the dog lives or dies, the act of maliciously wounding or mistreating a dog is a felony. And we've got to act! Really? But not for children?

But you've got to keep going. You've got to move to the third step. If you are going to murder them inside, then you are going to murder them outside, now you murder the defective children. How about if we just get rid of the ones we don't like. You know, those defective kids. And you are thinking, 'Oh, no!' Folks, this has already been going on for quite some time. I want to talk about it and expose it. It's a slippery slope. Because again, do you think it's going to stop? No! A little bit of sin spreads. A little bit of yeast, spreads. If you give it a foothold it isn't going to stop. And certainly, giving a foothold to murder isn't going to stop. One of the big reasons, and there are many reasons that they have come up with, but one of the big reasons why they want to kill children, specifically the ones they call defective, is the ones born with Down Syndrome. It's not the only one but it is one of the most popular.

Believe it or not, this has been going on for quite some time. Our daughter just turned 18, this happened with our daughter and our son, who is just turning 15. This happened 18 years ago. The doctor came in and said, 'We can run a test to see how your child is doing.' We were like…'What?' He said, 'Yes, to see if there are any defects, Down Syndrome, anything wrong with the child.' We replied, 'You can take that test and.... you be grateful we are Christians.' We were shocked. We said, 'NO! We will take any child God gives us because that child is from God. And God says all children are a blessing from Him, then He will entrust us with their care. They are a privilege, keep your test!' They are using this as a scare tactic in the abortion, i.e., murder of children movement, to get girls who are kind of waffling, unsure if they want the baby. But once they hear Down Syndrome, it scares them into doing it. I'm going to share with you an actual recorded phone call into an abortion clinic in New Mexico and watch how that is used as a scare tactic. You are also going to hear the price, thousands of dollars, and then you will hear, you better do it now because if you wait another week it's going up another thousand. Then you're going to hear, oh, don't worry we have a priest on hand who can help calm your spiritual fears. Here is the actual telephone conversation.

New Mexico True Reports: *"Southwestern Women's Clinic, how can I help you?*

Caller: *"Yes, I was wondering what services you offer. I am pregnant, my name is Bethany, and I am just wondering..."*

Women's clinic: *"We do pregnancy terminations here, what was the first day of your last normal period?"*

Caller: *"12/14/16"*

Women's Clinic: *"Do you know how far you think you are?"*

Caller: *"I'm 29 weeks, I believe."*

Women's Clinic: *"Okay, what state are you calling from?"*

Caller: *"I'm calling from Texas, Lubbock, Texas."*

Women's Clinic: *"Okay. So, what we do at this time of the pregnancy, for termination, is what we call it, induction procedure, it will require you to be in Albuquerque from a Monday afternoon or evening to a Friday afternoon or evening. We will spend a couple of days softening and dilating your cervix, and then we will induce labor. So, you will be going through active labor and delivery of a stillborn. Is there anything wrong with the pregnancy?"*

Caller: *"Well they said they found an anomaly."*

Women's Clinic: *"Did they tell you what they were?"*

Caller: "*They weren't sure, they thought maybe Down Syndrome and that kind of made me nervous because I don't really, I don't want to have, I'm afraid to deal with all of that.*"

Women's Clinic: "*Of course. That is a lifetime of commitment. We would be starting this procedure on the 11th. Now at that point in time, you would be looking at a $11,500.00 fee and the week after that, if we can't make it happen this week, we will be looking at a $12,500.00 fee.*"

No Gestational limits on abortion means that Southwestern Women's options will perform an abortion up to the day of birth on a disabled child.

Caller: "*My big concern is, I'm Catholic and religious. I would like to know if there is a possibility of having a priest there or how does that work? Do you even have that?*"

Women's Clinic: "*We work with an organization called the Religious Coalition for Reproductive Choice and believe it or not there is a priest affiliated with them, he has come here on numerous occasions. They are really wonderful, they are pro-choice, we work with them all the time. We don't know what we would do without them.*"

Wow, where do you even start? I was thinking of that price. But remember the further the baby is developed, the more money, and now she is far enough along that it's over ten thousand dollars. You are dealing with a good-sized child that they are going to dismember. $11,500 and if you don't do it this week, next week it's going up to $12,500. Don't tell me that's not a fear tactic. The Down Syndrome thing, 'Oh yeah, that's a commitment, you're doomed now.' Watching this again, what went through my mind was, there are hit men out there, or so I hear, never hired one in case you're wondering, that will kill people cheaper than that. Yet these guys get to do it, so called legally, and become millionaires, and it is okay. Hitmen go to jail, but these people don't. They made a business out of it. But again, it's sick, and then they have a guy that is supposed to represent the church, but as we know, Roman Catholicism is not the same thing as Biblical Christianity. If you have any questions about that, get our resource Roman Catholicism and the Coming World Religion.

That is sick, brutal, gross, but guess what? They get these diagnoses wrong all the time. Now it's wrong, don't misunderstand me. I don't care what the child has. You trust God and you be responsible. There is no reason to kill a child, but these guys get it wrong all the time. Or, are they really doing it on purpose? Here just one example of the wrong diagnosis.

Joshua Sheenan is a typical young baby – but during pregnancy when his mum Melanie went for her 20 weeks scan, she was told that her son had fatal foetal abnormalities and would not survive birth. Melanie and her husband Damien were then put under immense pressure to have an abortion.

Melanie Sheenan: "*We first became aware of those difficulties with the pregnancy at 20 weeks. We went to the radiographer and there was just silence. She wouldn't speak to us at all, she just said something is wrong. She wanted to contact a consultant, so she phoned him and brought him up to scan me. He told us he wasn't sure what he was dealing with and we had to be referred to a specialist hospital. They told us that there were severe abnormalities with the baby, the brain wasn't formed, the spine wasn't formed, it was so severe that they referred us to a hospital in Sheffield to do MRI's. We saw a few different consultants there and it was at that stage that they recommended an abortion.*

They felt that the child wouldn't survive birth and if it did, it would be so profoundly disabled, their words were, it would have no quality of life. They said his lungs wouldn't be fit to breath on his own.

From the first minute of life he has never needed resuscitation. He has never needed anything for breathing at all. They told us that his hydrocephalus would be so severe and that it would never be manageable. However, when he was born, he had no hydrocephalus at all. The doctors said, 'incompatible with life' and now he is 16 weeks old, he's brilliant, he's just a wee fighter. He is 16 weeks old and is completely age appropriate. He is doing everything that he should be doing."

Can somebody say he's a wee fighter? So, what's the point? I'm telling you that is just one of a multitude of examples of misdiagnosis. Doctors get it wrong all the time. But it wasn't just, hey, there's a problem here. It's, 'Hey, there's a problem here, your life will be doomed, you need to kill it.' That's the savagery. Again, it's wrong to murder any child but now it's where you need to get rid of those defective ones so your life isn't impugned. I received this email after our first study. This lady sent this to me. Her name was Linda.

She said, "*Pastor Billy, I want to thank you for your message on the mass murder of children. I just finished listening to part two and I'm shaking with disgust and heartbroken. I realize that part one is no longer on YouTube, but it looks like I may be able to listen to the rest of it on Facebook. But before I do that, can I share something with you?*

Two years ago, I believe my niece was 24 weeks pregnant with her second child, when she was told that there might be a possibility that her child could have Down Syndrome and she should consider aborting, i.e. murdering it. She didn't and today she has a beautiful, healthy, little girl. Thank you, Lord. But a few months ago, a friend of ours, a brother in the Lord, came over and he said his son and daughter-in-law were pregnant with their second child and were told that it was deformed and that they should consider abortion.

They unfortunately did. Our friend is devastated to say the least. After hearing both of these stories I started doing some research about abortion and found a lot of the same facts that you are presenting in your messages and also came to the conclusion that these people may very well be lying to mothers who are not willing to raise children with special needs.

Just my thought but I don't think I am wrong. Two young mothers in my circle, who I know were told that their babies were not heathy, and they were told they should consider killing it. Not a coincidence to me. Thanks again for your ministry as you continue to expose all the evil one's sick tactics."

In fact, to show you how sick it really is, we have to get rid of these kids not only in the womb, but now they are discussing outside the womb, and now we have gone to the third stage, let's get rid of the defective ones too. This is mind blowing. Here are the stats on just murdering Down Syndrome babies.

Right now, Iceland kills 99% of babies with Down Syndrome in abortion, Denmark 98%, France 77%, and the U.S. 67%. 67% of Down Syndrome babies are murdered in our country. Can we call that what it is? That is called Eugenics. And if you think that program has stopped, you're kidding yourself. Remember that was the backbone and background of Margaret Sanger who started Planned Parenthood. They never stopped that goal. But this is the global statistics. Let me read from this article.

"Last year CBS News reported that Iceland is close to eradicating Down Syndrome since prenatal screening has become available."

What they really mean is that people with Down Syndrome are being eradicated by selective abortion, or murder. Wasn't there somebody in history a few decades back that tried to eradicate a certain group of people? It rhymes with Hitler. Yet this is okay to eradicate children with Down Syndrome.

"Denmark is next with a 98% abortion count, France is 77%, United States 67%, this is a tragic loss for the whole world, and it is driven by fear. The first thing that parents hear when they find out their child has Down Syndrome in the medical industry is 'I'm so sorry' and then they give them a list of things that child will never do, never accomplish, your life is doomed.'" That is a lie.

"*The pressure to abort is always there. Children with Down Syndrome is not something to be afraid of. They bring love and joy, people with Down Syndrome break stereotypes every single day. Some today are models, chiefs, musicians, athletes, entrepreneurs, they are advocates, lobbyists, they even testify before Congress, some even get to go to the White House and meet the President.*

"I know a lot of people including myself, that never got to do that. Should we get rid of those folks? They have fulfilling jobs, busy social calendars, they have loving marriages, they have their own voices and dreams for the future and they never stop learning. In fact, research shows that 99% of people with Down Syndrome are happy with their lives. Some have challenges, of course, and need help at times, but who doesn't?"

So, what is next? Do you roll over and play dead on that one? Are you going to get rid of defective adults? I mean they need a lot of help too. They infringe on your time and it's not an easy procedure to have to take care of somebody like that. That's exactly where it is headed and that is for the next chapter. I like what this mom said to her a so-called doctor who encouraged her to murder her child who did have Down Syndrome.

Fox & Friends Reports: "*A mother's powerful message is going viral this morning. Courtney Baker's doctor suggested that she have an abortion because* *her baby had Down Syndrome. She refused and now that baby is 15 months old and she is beautiful. Mrs. Baker wrote to that doctor saying this.*

Courtney Baker: *"You were so very wrong to say a baby with Down Syndrome would decrease our quality of life... So, my prayer is that no other mommy will have to go through what I did. My prayer is that you, too, will now see true beauty and pure love with every sonogram."*

Amen, because what does the Scripture say? All children are a gift from God. Yeah, they are going to need some care, we're going to need some care. They need help, guess what, we all need help. They might fumble and make some mistakes. Have you ever made one? I'm telling you, it's a slippery slope, it's wrong through and through and we are at stage three. You're looking inside the womb, outside the womb and now you are getting selective. Starting with the defective ones, but they are not defective. Children with Down Syndrome can produce one of the greatest joys in life. But our society is so brutal and wicked they think it's the end of your life. Here's just one example of what we are missing out on with children with Down Syndrome.

"Emma is 10 and started to walk on her own in December when she was 9 years 8 months and 10 days, if anyone is counting. This was something that was just so awesome. If she was a regular kid and she walked at 18 months or 2 years, it would be like woohoo she walked. But I think seeing Emma walk, at that age, it is something that is so amazing. But also, it's a gift for other people too. I think it is just the coolest thing we get to see such small increments, small progress that we even sometimes take it for granted after she accomplished something. It's a gift that she gives us all.

"So, if you're a mom and you have just been told that you are going to have a child with special needs, it's not the end of the world. It's the beginning of a whole new world. It's an amazing adventure that you are going to be on, and there is an adventure to it, but there is a lot of joy and you get to experience so much about people that you would not have imagined how good people really are. Good days, 10-1, you work it out like any other problem, any other issue in your life. God will work it out. You cannot come first. And that goes with any parent. I don't care about the ability or disability of the child. You need to live for the kid. It's neat to know that they are the number one priority."

Because that is what God says to do. They are all a gift. Every child is different. I love his phrase; God will work it out. That's what parents are supposed to do. Just work it out like any other challenge. You work it out, you don't murder. Yet 67% in our own country murder, and 100% in other countries are selectively killing these children. You know what that is? It's savagery, it's brutal, it's anemeros. That's the last days society. So where does our society get this sick idea? It's not just okay to kill children, inside the womb, outside the womb, defective children, where does that come from? Margaret Sanger. Planned Parenthood, who we quoted before, get rid of those defective kids. They are like weeds. Right? From different races, who are impoverished. I am going to close this chapter with this. I can't believe I came across this. This is Margaret Sanger from back in the day, interviewed by Mike Wallace. It's a long interview, but I came across this one section. Watch what she calls the greatest sin of all. From the founder of Planned Parenthood.

Mike Wallace: "*Do you believe in sin? I don't mean do you believe in committing sin. I mean do you believe there is such a thing?*"

Margaret Sanger: "*I think the greatest sin in the world is bringing children into the world. They have disease from their parents, they have no chance in the world, they are delinquents, prisoners, and they are just marked when they are born. It's the greatest sin that people can commit.*"

Not murdering children, not selectively murdering children, but the greatest sin is even allowing them to come into existence. And oh, by the way, what is her solution to fix it? You kill them. This is not just sick, it is brutal, it's not just murder, it's not just infanticide, you are actually at that stage, and it came from the root and she got it from Hitler. We already saw this from history, and he got it from the lie of evolution, and all lies come from who? The father of all lies, satan, in John Chapter 8, he's a murderer and has been one since the beginning. We are talking full blown Eugenics, selective breeding. It's not coming, it's happening. We've been through three steps and they are going even further than this. Next, we're going to see the rationale, you roll over, you play dead, sin doesn't stop, it keeps infecting, it keeps spreading just like yeast, and if it's ok to kill kids inside the womb, and now we are having discussions outside the womb, and we already have horrid, brutal statistics that they are killing defective kids, then why not adults that are defective? That is exactly where it is headed and not only headed, but already being done. The next chapter is going to deal with assisted suicide, the Obamacare Death Panels, yes, they are in existence, the media mocks anyone, including Sarah Palin who actually mentioned this. We are also going to take a look at cloning people to harvest them for their organs and harvesting people alive for their organs. It's already being done on our planet and I have got proof.

Chapter Eight

The Future of Abortion Part 2

Last time we dealt with the first part of the future of abortion and we saw that if we don't speak up, it's not going to stop inside the womb. In fact, it's already happening in our own country. Right now, there is a discussion about not only murdering children inside the womb, outside the womb and where we left off, now it's going even further than that. Now how about we get rid of those kids that we deem as a society or by the medical community, defective? Now we are getting into the full blown what? Eugenics. Eu... meaning good, genics... meaning race or genes, a good race. But if they have defects then that's not a good race. Who does that sound like? It's Hitler. It's happening right now.

But again, they change the terminology. The Eugenics movement through abortion is still in high gear. Now we are going to see that it gets even worse than that. It's not only, as we saw before, creating that brutal, savage society, and murdering children certainly is brutally savage, but it is also leading to a murderously wicked society. The final stage that the book of Romans says that once you defy God you are going to reach that final stage of a depraved mind. And it's going to get absolutely wicked. Murder is going to go crazy, not just inside the womb but outside the womb and we are going to be next. Let's look at that final stage that God warned about 2,000 years ago. We are taking it full circle to end here. I'm convinced that we are in this final horrific stage.

In Romans Chapter 1, they had the audacity to say that there is no God and they worshiped things instead of the creator. They said that God doesn't exist even though He gave them plenty of evidence of his existence and of course that is what evolution does. And He says that once you give into that lie of evolution, you are set up to get into an extremely immoral society and we certainly have that. Then you are going to start condoning homosexuality and lesbianism, and we are certainly there. Then it gets to the final stage that Paul talks about in that slide, that once you turn away from God and you promote that in your society, this is where you are headed.

Romans 1:28-32: *"Furthermore, since they did not think it worthwhile to retain the knowledge of God, he gave them over to a depraved mind...*

Have you noticed that we are living in that last day? How can you even think that? How can that even come out of your mouth? What kind of a logic is that? Who in their right mind believes something like that? Or to promote something like that? Well, that is a depraved mind.

...to do what ought not to be done. They have become filled with every kind of wickedness, evil, greed and depravity. They are full of envy, murder, strife, deceit and malice. They are gossips, slanderers, God-haters...

These people who are pro-murdering children, and as we will see in this chapter, even pro-murdering adults, teenagers, kids, they hate God, it's the atheist mind-set.

...insolent, arrogant and boastful. They invent ways (of helping humanity, improving our condition?) *They invent ways of doing evil.* (They just can't get enough of it) *They disobey their parents; they are senseless, faithless, heartless, ruthless. Although they know God's righteous decree that those who do such things deserve death, they not only continue to do these very things but also approve of those who practice them."*

And we certainly saw that with the Supreme Court decision on homosexuality, they approved things, even in this context, God says, 'you better not do that,' it's going to get worse. But when it comes to this brutal society, inventing new ways of doing evil things, what's next? How many times have we said that? It's like they are inventing new ways. Now they are doing what? They are inventing new ways of doing evil. But it doesn't just say that they do that, it says that they *approve* of those who do these things. And that is going on in our world today. Basically, what we are seeing is the final stage, we have gone the full circle, this is where we started, believe it or not, when we opened up that Pandora's box of legalizing the murder of children inside the womb, you end up in this final stage. It's leading to murder, wholesale slaughter. In fact, the word in the Greek is literally the word for slaughter. It's not just murder, it's what is coming to our society in this final stage, it is wholesale slaughter. We see that to the tune of 60+ million children being murdered, but that's not just murder, it's slaughter.

But what we are going to deal with in this chapter, is that it is not going to stop there. You are going to see a wholesale slaughter of people outside the womb. This is the rationale because it is that slippery slope, that Pandora's box. We have rolled over and played dead by and large. The church is silent on this issue, so they are running with it. Well, if you have given us permission, (wink, wink), we haven't, I haven't, but in our country, they gave us permission to murder children inside the womb, now this is the discussion, well, we now murder them outside the womb. Let's get rid of those defective kids as well. Again, this is their logical progression. If we can have a wholesale slaughter of those young people, hey, why not adults? Especially if you are going down that defective route. I mean adults have defections. They have problems. Why can't we just get rid of them? This is where they are headed. They are going to invent new ways, not to just kill children in the womb, they are going to invent new ways, and might I say, those ways are now in place to murder adults.

They are going to have facilities, just like abortion facilities, they are going to have murder facilities to murder adults. To get rid of your defective loved one. That is an oxymoron. Let's take my loved one and kill them. And then of course the government is going to get involved. It will be a service you can pay for, if you can believe that, we are even having this discussion, like you can pay to have a child murdered, now they are going to have these facilities where you can pay to have an adult murdered. And nobody goes to jail for it. Then it's looked upon as something patriotic. Something that is a good thing to do. Which again is what euthanasia means. *Eu*, good, *thanasia*, death. Good death, it's a good thing to do. And then of course, at first, it will be voluntary, but when the government gets hold of it, then the government will decide who will live and who will die. What does that sound like? It sounds like a bunch of science fiction movies. Take your pick, *Solvent Green*, or *Logan's Run*, you are going to see people right now in the news, that we need to die by the age of 75.

I found this cassette that I acquired about 15 to 20 years ago where Dr. Dobson from *Focus on the Family* was interviewing Dr. Bernard Nathanson and he warned of what is coming because we are not stopping abortion. Here's just a little bit of his background, and then I'll give a transcript of the broadcast and you will see that everything he warned about 15-20 years ago is happening right now. It's shocking and gross.

Who is Dr. Bernard Nathanson? He is the guy that helped usher in the barbaric age of abortion on demand. The most atrocious holocaust in the history of the world. He was the founder of the National Association for Repeal of Abortion Laws. He was the one that I quoted before who fabricated the numbers that women were dying by the 1,000's from illegal abortions, he was the one who paved the way for the passing of Roe vs Wade. It says here that at his funeral, it was filled with pro-life activists even though he was responsible for more than 75,000 deaths at the largest abortion facility in the world. Well, what happened?

Even before he got saved, he came across ultrasounds. It helped him to see what pro-lifers knew. Meaning, that is a human being inside the womb. He committed his last abortion in 1979. So shortly after, being the big guy that got Roe vs Wade passed, he come across this, and he quit. He's wasn't a Christian, but he knew enough to quit. Certain that it would convince others that abortion destroys a human being that can feel pain, he produced the film, *Silent Scream* which showed the aborting of a 12-week baby. He said, as the baby recoils from the deadly instrument, it opens its mouth. This is the silent scream of a child threatened with imminent destruction, as it is killed in the womb. What was cool, at that time, was that Ronald Reagan hoped this would change minds, so he showed this at the White House. And guess who is showing a pro-life video at the White House here real soon? President Trump. He is showing 'Gosnell', Praise God for that! In 1987 Dr Nathanson came out with this film, *The Eclipse of Reason.* It explains abortion procedures; it shows the murder of a 5-month-old baby and then interviews the ladies and they give their testimonies of how it

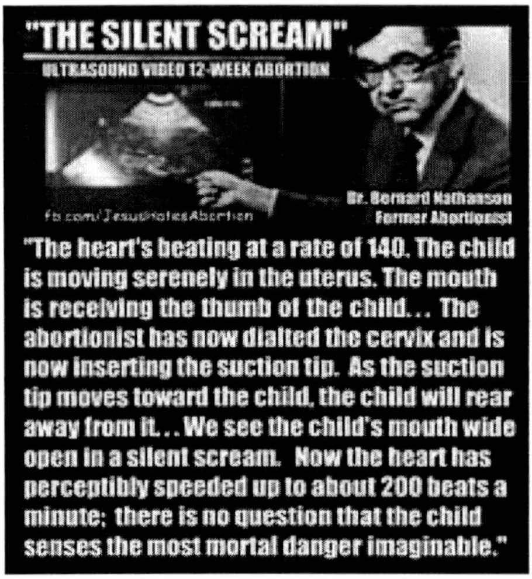

destroyed their lives. Now, he was still not saved, but he was the biggest proponent of pro-life because this is wrong. But in 1996, basically 20 years after he already turned around and stopped doing this, he finally got saved. He was a Jewish atheist and he became a Christian. He wrote about his life in a book titled *The Hand of God.* There he tells what turned him to Christ was the Christians he

saw who witnessed and spoke up at abortion clinics. He said that while he was in the Air Force he had attended a Bible Study and he found that the New Testament God was a loving and forgiving figure whom he could seek and ultimately find the forgiveness that he had pursued so hopelessly for so long. And he found out that he could be forgiven for what he had done, the deaths of 75,000 children. He said he was witnessed to by the pro-life demonstrators that were willing to suffer scorn, and even jail and bankruptcy. He said they prayed, supported and encouraged each other, they sang hymns of joy and constantly reminded each other of the absolute prohibition against murdering unborn children. That had a huge impact on him. In the book *The Hand of God* he said, this is where it is heading. Now what he says speaks volumes. He was the one that helped get Roe vs Wade passed, he was there. What he said was going to happen is if we do not shut down abortion it will lead to, not just euthanasia, murdering adults, it is going to lead to an industrial euthanasia. There will be centers to go to, just like abortion clinics that murder children, there will be centers in our society launched all around the world to take a person to kill them. This is what he warned us about. This is what he said in his book, *The Hand of God.*

"Drawing largely from my experience with a similar brand of pagan access, I predict that entrepreneurs will set up multiple discreet infirmaries for those who wish or have been talked into or coerced into or medically deceived into killing themselves." That will only be the first phase. And then he throws out a name. He said, "*They will probably call it a thanatoria or thanatorium.*" Again, the Greek work for death is Thanatos. He says, "*They will expand into chains. And then accountants will eventually assume command, handling expenses and overhead as competition grows. Finally, streamlined and efficient, the flawless*

version of the thanatorium will resemble the assembly line factories that the abortion clinics have become and farther on down the slope the ovens of Auschwitz."

So basically, what he warned against 15-20 years ago, was that if we don't put a stop to abortion, here is your future. It's going to result in an industry to take adults to, to kill them, which is the same thing, in essence, to what Hitler did to the Jewish people, except this one is legalized by the government. At first it will be voluntary but eventually even that will be taken away. He died on February 21, 2011 of cancer, but his life, his testimony, and the power of God's Grace is the power of truth and it is the profound encouragement that just as God created us he can recreate any one of us no matter the depth of our sin. So that is a message of hope. But here it is, of what he warned about on tape with Dr. Dobson and it gets freaky. As I'm listening to it, I am thinking I can't believe it made it on the air.

Dr. Dobson: *"Can you comment on this? You use the word euthanasia for so long that you have made me sensitive about it. How do you see that issue and where it's going and what is its impact going to be?"*

Dr. Nathanson: *"I have said it in my book, and I will say it here. In the beginning there will be refined, dignified, quiet, places that may be called thanatoriums or some fancy word like that, where you will take your grandfather who is suffering from terminal cancer. They will be very understanding, and they will kill him, but in a very quiet, dignified way. That of course will cost money, but that will go on in these little private infirmaries that are not going to be covered by insurance.*

"That will go on until the accountants and the bean counters get hold of this thing because it will be a cash business, like the abortion business, which is heavily infiltrated by organized crime anyway. So, the bean counters and organized crime and accountants that get hold of these things, they will spring up and the next thing you know they aren't going to be so clean and so nice and so quiet. They are going to be like factories where they can get rid of them in a minute.

"This is where the abortion clinics have gone. It's going to be a terrible, dehumanizing, disgusting industry. They will try to regulate it, but they will not be able to because it can be done in a doctor's office as well as in clinics. And

eventually it will end up exactly the same as abortion has, in the hands of a relatively small number of entrepreneurs who are making a fortune off of dead little babies and have no respect for life at all. And that's what is going to happen in that area."

Dr. Dobson: "*What else in that area stirs in your soul?"*

Dr. Nathanson: *"Well, Dr. Dobson, I had an eye opener in my year in Georgetown in bioethics, then I switched over to Vanderbilt for 2 ½ years, specializing in bioethics and we talked some about abortion. We talked about the act of killing and assisted suicide and all the rest of it, but what struck me as the most dangerous threat on the horizon is the ethics of genetic manipulation and engineering. People say to me this is science fiction, why are you talking about science fiction?*

"I had a priest say this to me a couple weeks ago in Mexico City. If 30 or 40 years ago someone would have said to me 'we are going to create babies in test tubes' I would have said, 'what are you crazy, you need to be locked up.' But I'm telling you, this is not science fiction. They are preparing for, one, immortality, somatic immortality on this earth. We are going to be living 1,000 years because the aging process has now been defined genetically. We have located the gene that is responsible for aging.

"And there is every reason to believe that these genes are going to be deactivated. And we are never going to age. The second thing they are doing is that they are preparing to launch a new species. They are fortifying the intelligence genes. They are reducing other genes and they are going to make a new species of person. Super persons with super intelligence and persons with no intelligence but have brute animal genes so they are very strong, and they will do all the menial jobs. You and I and everyone else here probably, we will be kept as pets. Household pets."

Dr. Dobson: "*That is frightening."*

15-20 years ago, he warned about that. I don't have time to get into the genetic alteration thing, but that is also going on. Basically, as you saw, Hollywood is doing a good job of preparing us for creating super humans with the Marvel movies and X-Men. That is going on right now. That goes along with what he said 15-20 years ago on a *Focus on the Family* broadcast. The guy who headed up and got Roe vs Wade passed, who later stopped, and later became a Christian. He warned that this is the future. That you open Pandora's Box, that you roll over and allow the murder of children inside the womb, it's going to move outside the womb, and not just children, defective children outside the womb, but defective adults and it's going to become an industry. So, that aspect is what I want to hone into in this chapter.

That industry, as he said, thanatoriums, to take your elderly there and get rid of them. To become a cash-cow like the abortion industry, that is already being done. It's being done as we speak. Again, the word euthanasia means 'good death.' They do the same thing when it comes to abortion. The people that are for abortion, they hide behind their terminology. They say, 'Do you mean you are against pro-choice?' Yes, I'm against anybody choosing to murder a child. Remember we said you can't use their terms; we have to retell it because they hide behind it. They do the same thing with euthanasia. That is a fetus, no that is a child. That is a blob of tissue, no that is a child, that is just a pregnancy termination, no you just murdered a child. Euthanasia does the same thing, because it is the same death culture. They want to say that euthanasia is a 'good death.' It's not a 'good death.' You will see that in some of the words they use in print. They call it mercy killing, physician assisted suicide, and imposed death. Translate it for what it is. When you see the term euthanasia, it is murdering adults. When you see the term, physician assisted suicide, it is a doctor who helped somebody kill them themselves. And you will see that even 'choice' will be taken away from that person. Mercy killing, there is nothing merciful about it. You committed a crime. You murdered somebody. This is the final stage of the Romans 1 warning from God, and now you put this together with the murdering of 60+million children, just in the United States.

Now you add to this death culture that is coming, of wholesale slaughter outside, that is what the Greek word means, slaughter, in the last days. If you keep going down this route your whole world is going to slaughter itself. And that's what's coming. That is the future of abortion. Now supporters will say, 'We're here to help the individual who is suffering to die with dignity.' There is nothing dignified in helping somebody to self-murder which is what suicide is. That's what is going on so don't fall for it. Today we hear about euthanasia in the health care context. And just so you know, euthanasia is not administering medication that is needed to control pain. If a person is suffering, that is called normal good medical care. That's not what euthanasia means. Euthanasia means to intentionally bring someone's death. There's nothing merciful about it. First you are killing that child in the womb, now you are killing that adult. Now you are going to see it's getting even lower in age. Teenagers are being knocked off and even young children. We'll get to that shortly. Euthanasia, assisted suicide, is murder, that's all it is. You might wonder how did we cross the line on this? This is a social taboo. Who would create facilities to kill them off? It's already happening and again, it's a Pandora's Box. If you roll over and play dead with what's going on inside the womb, it's going to happen outside the womb as well. That's the future of abortion.

As we saw before, little by little, it's called soft disclosure, because if you appear on the scene and say, "Hey we want to create thanatoriums, we want to create another industry of death and make millions and billions of dollars off of killing adults," now, you would freak! So, you slowly but surely get them used to the idea, you twist the terminology, oh, it's not murdering an adult, it's dying with dignity. Oh, who could be against that? No, it's murdering an adult. They are doing the same thing. Now, one of the guys that really began to crack it was Dr. Jack Kevorkian. Remember that guy? When it first came out, people were saying, 'This guy is nuts. He's crazy, lock him up in jail!' Did you know, to date, he has on record, killed 130 people? Not 1, not 30, but 130 people. He was the one that basically, at first, got people freaked out. But he got the idea going. It's called soft disclosure. They said that you have to oppose this because what it will lead to eventually is they will create these facilities and at first you get to make the choice, but then that choice will be taken away from you, it will be taken away from the loved ones making the choice for you. We are already at that stage. Then the government will decide. When you live and when you die. Another one that they have, it's called a movement. You had the 'abortion movement', now it's the 'right to die movement.' 'You mean to tell me you are against the right to die?' I'm against helping adults kill themselves. And I'm really against taking away the choice of adults to kill themselves. They shouldn't do it anyway because again, suicide is murder, and murder is wrong. Murder is a sin and you just did it to yourself. It's wrong, of course I'm against that. But again, that is

what they do, they hide behind the terminology. Believe it or not, this has been going on for a long time. When you look back at history it was going on in Greece and Rome in the fourth century B.C. They had something that was still in existence until about 30 years ago. It was called the Hippocratic Oath. The Hippocratic Oath was by the Father of Medicine, Hippocrates. Believe it or not, everybody in medicine had to sign off, they had to take the Hippocratic Oath when they became a doctor. And even back then in the fourth century he said, "*I will please no one and I will not prescribe a deadly drug or give advice that may cause his death. Nor will I give a woman a device to procure an abortion.*" Even back then that was part of the Hippocratic Oath. And we see now they are doing both. They are violating that very oath.

So, lets back up a little bit to pre-Kevorkian and show you how this death culture can now murder an adult outside the womb, which is an extension of eugenics from Hitler that is in full swing today. It did not die out with Hitler. It continued with Margaret Sanger, still to this day, with the Planned Parenthood industry, but now it continues with the adults which made it outside the womb with the euthanasia movement. In 1938, who was rising to power? The Euthanasia Society was founded in New York. Is New York a liberal state? You are going to see a parallel between the Democrat Party, the Death Party, which is for the complete termination of children all the way up to birth but guess who is also promoting killing people outside the womb? Democrats. That was founded in 1938 and listen to their stated goal right out of the gates. "*To gain social and legal acceptance, the right to kill vulnerable human beings.*" You think, well that is a loaded term. Well, they define it. *"People the organization called mental, defective and incurables."*

Did you know that there is terminology in the press saying that you and I as evangelical Christians are mentally deficient? That we have a mental religious disorder? In Europe there is a terminology, in print, when they are in the courts, they are saying they want to outlaw what we call sharing the Gospel because that is a form of mental manipulation on somebody else. So again, the power of those words, mental, defective and incurables, who gets to define that? You would think it is just somebody with a brain deficiency, they can say you are mentally defective, and we need to get rid of you. But that was at its conception in our own country in New York in 1938. Then in 1939 they made their first attempt to legalize euthanasia, but it didn't get much headway so they changed tactics. They sat back for several decades, then they went into the medical industry and the educational industry to get their terminology equipped and change the mind of the people. In 1967 they had launched a massive educational campaign, and this was when they introduced their first foot in the door. Their words, "*This will be a foot in the door for the social and legal acceptance of euthanasia.*" And that was the beginning of the 'The Living Will.' Because if they can have you sign off on that, then that is the first crack in the door and you're not going to wait for natural circumstances. We'll help you. And that's their foot in the door back in 1967.

Then in 1968 and 1973 they unsuccessfully tried to get the right to die legislation passed in Florida. Now you can see they are not just educating but now they are attacking the court system. At first, they aren't getting anywhere, but once they get that crack in the door, today it is going crazy. The flood gate has been opened. But back in 1968 and 1973 when they were pushing this through Florida, there was a guy named Walter Sackett, a pro-euthanasia doctor. He said this would save millions of dollars if the states mongoloids, a non-politically correct term for Down Syndrome, were permitted to succumb to pneumonia. He even tells you why they need to die. These people don't deserve to live. Let them go. Let them die of pneumonia. We don't need to give them care; we're going to help them die. That's euthanasia.

Then in 1973 they had a big breakthrough. Roe vs Wade. Now they could have facilities to murder children, and adults are next. The very next year, a guy names Joseph Fletcher took over as the president of the ESA. He is known as the father of situation ethics. Have you heard of that term? This is the guy that started that. He was a professor and an Episcopal Priest who later renounced his belief in God. Oh, he lost his salvation. No, he was never saved.

1 John 2:19 says, "The reason they went out from us is they never belonged to us. If they belonged to us, they would have remained with us, but they are gone so none of them belonged to us."

He was a fake, as we saw before. Here is his mantra, this is the father of situation ethics about bringing in this death culture and murdering adults. He said, "*What has taken place in birth control,* (meaning you have accepted that now) *is equally important in death control.*" You start on one side and it opens up on the other. "*Based on the notion that there are now no fixed moral laws* (they got rid of the Ten Commandments) *now one can make exceptions for killing unwanted unborn children, people who are suffering, the elderly or handicapped or those who are burdens on others.*" Which included health care, with prices that were skyrocketing. We need to get rid of those people who are costing too much. In 1975 they changed their name to 'The Society For The Right to Die.' Why? Because they were concerned that the word euthanasia was reminiscent of the Nazi killing program and it might be hindering their success. They admit that they had to change names because people were equating it with eugenics and Hitler. And rightly so. Then in 1976 they had a huge breakthrough in California. Is that sort of a Democratic/ liberal state? That is when the Natural Death Act became the law. Again, back to legal wills. Now it's not just an option, now you have to. They have it now in one state and the push is to get it legalized in every state. They have their foot in the door to legalize it.

Then the Supreme Court in New Jersey decided the first right to die case. Now we are going to put it into action. Do you see the slow step by step process? Let's put it into action so now we can start murdering adults. Then we can equate that to being merciful to them. The first big one was Karen Ann Quinlan in 1976, who had severe brain damage. They killed her. This was an important breakthrough of conditioning. The court implied that the decision of another person to refuse treatment for an incompetent patient was the same as the patients' decision. They are at the point now that she did not ask to die, but they called it physician assisted suicide. This is a case, even back then, that she didn't make that choice. Somebody made that choice for her. This step went a long way in obliterating the distinction between voluntary and involuntary euthanasia, a huge breakthrough.

In 1980 they created what they called the Hemlock Society. Derek Humphry was a British journalist who moved to the U.S. with his second wife. Well, what happened to his first wife? I kid you not, in 1975 he helped his first wife kill herself by poisoning her morning coffee, then he wrote a book about it called 'Jeans Way.' And he didn't go to jail. He killed his wife. What is the Hemlock Society's purpose? To promote death on demand without restrictions. It

is named after the poison Hemlock that the ancient Greeks used in assisted suicides. In 1980 you have the World Federation of the Right to Die Society. Now they are branching out, going across the world. In 1984 you have Dr. Helga Kuhse who says, "*If we can get people to accept the removal of all treatments and care, especially the removal of food and fluid, they will then see what a painful way that is to die. Then in the patients' best interest, they will accept lethal injection.*"

They signed off and said they didn't want any care. That is how my grandmother died, in fact I will never forget, the medical staff chewed us up and down because my grandmothers' lips were so parched, and we were giving her ice chips. She was dying. They said you can't do that, it's against the law. Starvation and dehydration are the worst ways to die. And yet that is supposed to be mercy killing? A dignified way to die? No, it's not. But that is their first step. A Living Will, then the option, then it will be demanded by the states, then we won't let these people have food and water, but that's a horrible way to die, let's inject them now. It's a step by step process.

Then in 1985 three hundred people from all over the U.S. gathered together at the 2nd Annual Voluntary Euthanasia Conference sponsored by the Hemlock Society and here are some of the many issues that they discussed. How can active euthanasia be brought about? The suggestion was we can use a plastic bag light sedation. That is sick. Put a bag over their heads and give them some morphine, that will get rid of them. And get some money for doing it for you. For being merciful. Does giving a person the information on committing suicide constitute committing a crime? And should children have the right to choose euthanasia or suicide? They also said they were going to get this to the doctors as well, with money.

In 1987 they had another big breakthrough. 32-year-old Nancy Ellen Jobes was killed by dehydration after the New Jersey Supreme Court upheld lower court decisions, even though two neurologists found that Nancy was aware, responsive and purposeful, and they still killed her.

In 1988 you have The Americans Against Human Suffering. Now notice how they keep changing the terminology. Who's against human suffering? You mean you are against the rights to protect people from human suffering? Yes, I'm against the right of you people killing people! They are hiding behind the terminology, that's all it is! You killed children in the womb, now you want to kill adults. This is when they began to form the legalization of physician aid in dying.

In 1989 the Hemlock Society moved from California to Oregon. Now is Oregon a wonderful conservative place to live? No, it's not. Their goal is to gain social and legal acceptance for euthanasia by the removal of all medical treatment and care, mainly food and fluids, and action by lethal injection whether or not the patient has expressed a wish to die. They didn't do a Living Will, they didn't say, 'I want to die.' So now you're going to make their decision for them?

Then we get to 1990 when this guy is back. Jack Kevorkian hooked up the first one, Janet Atkins, to his self-execution machine. She was an Oregon woman in early stages of Alzheimer's. Criminal charges against him were dropped and the judge said, 'Don't use that machine again.' He invented that machine, invented ways of doing evil. Can you imagine somebody just shot a person in cold blood and the judge says, 'Don't do that again with that gun.' And they go free. That's what happened with this guy. Then he goes on his killing spree.

Also, in 1990 the U.S. Supreme Court decides its first right to die case and it concluded that the state may supply evidence in proceedings where the guardian seeks discontinuing nutrition and hydration of a person diagnosed to be in a persistent vegetative state. Next, in 1990, A Patient Self Determination Act was passed that forces all health care facilities and programs to promote advance directive for health care and if you don't comply you will be penalized by loss of Federal Funds, such as Medicare reimbursement. So, they forced them with the money and now it is a law. In 1991 they introduced the Society for the Right to Die and changed their name to The Choice in Dying.

They started pushing it through Washington and it was rejected. In 1992 they pushed it in California, and it was rejected. But again, they are getting closer each time. How many times did they approach the states with legalizing homosexual marriage? Tons of times, for many years. Finally, what happened? It cracked. The same thing happened with this, as we are going to see. Finally, in 1993, in Washington State, they developed Compassion in Dying to counsel the terminally ill to help them with personal assistance to hasten their death. So now, if you can't come to that conclusion on your own, we are going to bring in a panel of people, sit down with you and say you need to die.

In 1994, Oregon finally got it through. It narrowly passed but it got through. The Death with Dignity Act. Then every state enacted some type of act of advance directive, a major victory for the Right to Die Movement. Then by

1999 Jack Kevorkian had reached 130 people that he had killed. In 2000, The Choice in Dying changed their name to Partnership in Caring. The Hemlock Society, in 2003, changed their name to End of Life Choices. Then in 2004, Compassion in Dying, headquartered in Oregon, and End of Life Choices, which was formerly the Hemlock Society, headquartered in Denver, a huge liberal New Age place, merged together and now combined their work and are called Compassionate Choices.

At about this time there was another breakthrough that was a big deal in our country, the case was Terri Schiavo. Who decided that she should die? The courts. The Courts gave permission, legally, that you have to honor the husband's wishes. Was that her wish? No. So the courts said legally she has to die. That was a huge, huge, breakthrough and she was denied all food and water until she died, which is a horrible death. In 2006, Oregon State ruled in favor of Oregon's now Physicians Assisted Suicide Law. In 2008, Washington State voters passed the Death with Dignity Law. In 2009, Montana's Supreme Court affirmed the Physician Assisted Suicide Law. In 2013, Vermont now becomes the 4th state to pass the Death with Dignity Law. In 2014, New Mexico rules in favor of physicians to help patients end their lives and prohibits the prosecution of physicians, so now you can't send somebody to jail who murdered an adult. That would be against the law. Also, in 2014, Brittany Maynard died after moving from California to Oregon where in that state she had the right to die. She was protected by law and they put her to death. Do you see the trail? You roll over and play dead and it becomes a legal right to kill children, then the same death culture that God warned about in the final stages of a depraved mind, they are going to do the same thing to adults. It's eugenics in high gear. Now, it just so happens that not too long ago, California has now passed the physician assisted suicide.

CBN News.com: *"California is now the 5th state in the U.S. to legalize assisted suicide. Monday, Governor Jerry Brown signed a bill where terminally ill patients can legally end their lives using doctor prescribed drugs. The bill requires the patient to be capable of taking the medication themselves and two*

doctors have to approve it. But opponents say the bill legalizes premature suicide."

Marilyn Golden: "*People need to know that where suicide is legal some people's lives will be lost without their consent through mistakes and abuse. No safeguards have ever been enacted or even proposed that can prevent that outcome which can never be undone."*

CBN News.com: *"At least 24 other states have introduced right to die legislation this year."*

How many states? 24. It's the same thing as homosexuality. It took years and years and when they finally got their foot in the door, what happened? It exploded. The same thing is going on right now. To murder adults outside the womb, the right to do that, and I'm telling you that right will be taken away from that individual. It's wrong to do that anyway. Suicide is self-inflicted murder. It's wrong. Of course, this just happened last week. California, Oregon, Washington, all these liberal states, and New Jersey decided to do it too.

WJ reports: "*New Jersey Governor signs bill legalizing assisted suicide for terminally ill. Democratic New Jersey Governor Phil Murphy signed a bill Friday legalizing assisted suicide for persons who are terminally ill. The 'Medical Aid in Dying for the Terminally Ill Act' passed the state Assembly on March 25 by a vote of 41-33. The state Senate approved the legislation in a 21-16 vote."*

Governor Phil Murphy: "*Today's bill signing will make NJ the eighth state to allow terminally ill patents the dignity to make their own end-of-life decision – including medical aid in dying. We must give these patients the humanity, respect, and compassion they deserve."*

WJ Reports: *"Under the new law, patients must be older than 18, terminally ill and fully capable of making an informed decision. They may self-administer lethal medication only after counseling and officially requesting medication from a licensed physician. The new law comes after the American Academy of Family Physicians announced in October 2018 that it no longer opposes physician-assisted suicide, instead taking a neutral position. California, Vermont, Washington, Colorado, Hawaii, Oregon and the District of Columbia all have 'aid in dying' laws permitting terminally ill patients to commit suicide with the* *help of a physician. Assisted suicide in the Netherlands is legal for anyone who suffers from physical or mental illness and has an advanced directive or has received parental consent if they are younger than 16. New Jersey's law will take effect on August 1, 2019."*

Wow, they are getting younger, aren't they? Right now, in our country there are 9 states that say yes, we can now kill your adult, that's our culture now. California, Colorado, District of Columbia, Hawaii, Montana, Oregon, Washington, Vermont, and then starting August 1st of this year, New Jersey. By the way, it is the rage amongst the Democrats because this just came out also:

"Cuomo pushes for assisted suicide bill after New Jersey passes similar law."

Do you see the flood gates opening? It's the same state that says it's perfectly fine to kill a child all the way up to birth. Now they say they want to kill adults too. You wonder why and I'll say it again, the Democrat party is the Death Party. They want to kill children, and now they want to kill adults. This is sick! But this is the world we live in today. Now it is spreading across the world. Assisted suicide, murder of adults is legal in Belgium, Australia, China, Canada, Columbia, Denmark, Germany, Iceland, Ireland, Luxemburg, the Netherlands, New Zealand, South Africa, Switzerland, Uruguay, United Kingdom and of course the United States. But now, if we kill children inside and outside the womb, and we get to this spectrum where we can kill the supposedly elderly people, but forget that, how about just anybody that wants to die? How about we kill kids too. That is already going on. Here are some headlines.

'Children are being euthanized in Belgium.'

What does that mean? Children are being murdered in Belgium.

"Children ages 9 to 11 have been euthanized in Belgium. They were given lethal injections in the European country that permits children to choose to die with

terminal illnesses. Belgium has given lethal injections to a 17-year-old who was suffering from muscular dystrophy, a 9-year-old who had a brain tumor, and an 11-year-old who had cystic fibrosis."

What? So now it's not even terminal stuff. If you don't like the shape your body is in, we'll kill you even if you are a kid. This is sick! This is a wholesale slaughter of people!

"They were the first children under the age of 12 to be euthanized anywhere. Belgium changed its euthanasia law in 2014 giving doctors the legal right to terminate the life of the child no matter how young the patient was."

So, they may even go earlier. One guy who defended it said, *"I saw the mental and physical suffering. I thought we did a good thing."* Euthanasia, a good death. That is sick. A good thing, you killed 3 kids. Good thing it's not coming over here! Wrong. It's already happening in Canada. It hopped the pond already. Here are the headlines from Canada.

"Canadian Doctors Get Ready for Child Euthanasia." "A race for the once unthinkable is now accelerating."

Their argument is that there is no logical argument for limited euthanasia to adults. After all, children suffer too. Euthanasia has popular support in the Netherlands. Infanticide is openly practiced by Dutch doctors over there and they also promote that disabled babies can be killed. Now Canada seems to be on the verge of letting children be euthanized, i.e. murdered. That development is especially alarming for the United States given that Canada is our closest cultural cousin. Now, *"some parents in Canada are open to having their sick children killed."* How sick is that? As a parent you take care of your child. You don't say, this is too much of a burden for me, let's kill them. I should have a right for that. It's happening and how is that any different than the argument that they use for abortion, murdering your child? This child in the womb is a burden to me. I don't have time to take care of it. You kill it. Now they are doing the same thing outside. It's not coming, it's already here. Oh, and by the way, that's if the parent even knows about it or wants to go along with it. How about this headline:

CBN News: "*Toronto Hospital Releases Assisted Suicide Plan for Kids, May not Even Inform Parents." "Toronto's hospitals for sick children revealed that in* *some cases the young person's parents will not be notified of the intention to end their own lives until after the death is confirmed."*

A person warned this. "*When a culture differentiates when lives are worth living and lives are worth ending, there are consequences, the young, the old, the sick or disabled are disastrous. We all know that in Canada, an ER visit for a frail elderly person means lying on a gurney in the hallway for hours. That is the last place a dying person would want to be. This is the kind of humiliation that we should be ashamed of."*

So, let's kill them. You created the problem, didn't you? You created a government health care system that people have to wait forever, even if they are suffering. But now you say, let's not improve it, let's not get more doctors, let's not open up more facilities so we don't have to wait so long, let's just get rid of them. Let's kill them. That's not going to happen here is it? Of all places for this next article to appear, this was in the Washington Times, which is not known to be a conservative paper.

Washington Times reports: *"Saving money but costing lives, the Obamacare death panel should be killed before it's too late. In the Obamacare law..."*

By the way, the government has taken over our healthcare, and what is one of the Democrats big talking points for the next election? We need Healthcare for all. The government should take care of all our medical needs. And these are the same guys that want to kill children inside the womb and adults, outside. Do you think there is a plan? But even in this paper they admitted that in the existing healthcare plan, Obamacare, there are these things called death panels. Now Republicans did speak up back in the day, Sarah Palin did, but anybody that said there are death panels in there, they were laughed at and mocked. But now I guess they have realized that they really are in there.

Bill Akins, Pasco County Republican Party: "*Here is the problem I have with the Affordable Health Care Act. #1, there is a provision in there that anyone over the age of 74 has to go before what is effectively a death panel."* The crowd boos at him. *"Yes, they do, it's in there, folks. You're wrong!"*

Sarah Palin, Former GOP Vice-Presidential Nominee: "*Of course there are death panels in there, but the important thing to remember is that this is just one* *aspect of this atrocious, unaffordable, cumbersome, burdensome, evil policy of Obama, that is Obamacare."*

FOX News Reports: *"What do you think their motive is for coming onto your side, saying maybe we should slow down with this law?*

Sarah Palin: "*Well, it's black and white in the law that there will be rationing of health care. They couldn't go forever without acknowledging that or they would look like complete buffoons, and they would be deemed incompetent having not read the law to understand that death panels are a part of this atrocity."*

Barbara Walters: "*President Obama stood before one session of Congress and said there is no such thing as a death panel. Is he a liar?"*

Sarah Palin: *"He's not that, those two words will not be found in any of those thousands of pages of different variations of the health care bill. No, death panel isn't there. But he is incorrect, and he is disingenuous."*

RT News Reports: *"Dr. Ezekiel Emmanuel was one of the architects of the Affordable Care Act or in other words, Obamacare. He presumes to be interested in preserving life which is why it seemed outrageous when Sarah Palin accused him of creating death panels. That was him, the death panel guy. But it turned out that Palin may have been more right than the country gave her credit for because Dr. Emanuel just penned an article in the Atlantic titled, 'Why I hope to die at 75,' with a sub-title of, 'An argument that societies and families and you will be better off if nature takes its course, quickly and promptly.'*

In it, Emanuel clearly outlines why he thinks everyone should have the decency to die before turning 76. He accuses Americans with the obsession with trying to cheat death. He chastises people for exercising, for doing mental puzzles, sticking to healthful diets, or taking supplements, as though those actions were evil.

He said all those death cheating behaviors are part of a manic cultural type that he called the American Immortal which he rejects as misguided and destructive, destructive as in if you spend medical and financial resources trying to extend the life of a 76-year-old, you are being destructive to society. Sounds pretty death panel there."

Again, they are hiding behind the terminology, everybody said if you really read this healthcare bill, remember, 'We have to pass it so we can read what is in it', remember that from Nancy Pelosi? The words, death panel, are not in there, but that's what it is, and now this guy who authored this, it's now what he is saying what it is actually called, because 'death panel' would freak people out. It's called the IPAB or the Independent Payment Advisory Board. This is again from the Washington Times.

"Buried deep within the Obamacare is a provision that takes away healthcare from you and your doctors by taking away payment for critical healthcare that may be needed to save your life. The IPAB Board will be independent of you, your doctors, your hospitals, medical, Congress, Judiciary, credit process and ultimately the Constitution itself.

"The Keto institute warned us 5 years ago that the IPAB is independent in the worst sense of the word. Being independent of the Congress, the President, Judiciary, and the independent will of the people. Medicare spending is projected to grow faster than the economic growth data and it grows every year.

"Obamacare has left the IPAB with just two options. 1) You slash payments to doctors, hospitals and other healthcare providers under Medicare in order to survive the increase prices, which means they aren't going to get their care anyway and they might die *or 2) You deny specific healthcare treatments to seniors on the grounds that they are not cost effective, just like the British National Health Service does with the socialized medicine so admired by the Democrats."*

Do you see the slippery slope that is in there? Again, they authorize Obamacare to not limit the IPAB from cutting Medicare and authorizes them to maintain or enhance beneficiary access to quality care under Medicare.

In other words, they control whether you get that surgery or not. You know what, you lived a good life. Let's help you die with dignity. You're costing the system too much money. It's your patriotic duty to die. 15-20 years ago, what did Dr. Nathanson say? They will call them thanatoriums. You take that elderly person there. It's your patriotic duty to get rid of them. They are costing the system too much money. This is going on right now. What's weird is, the people that were for this, those involved in population control, Agenda 21, basically the elite that want to eliminate 90% of the population of the planet, and of course, it's never their family, it's always someone else's family. Well, one of those elites that we talked about before who is always big on population control is Bill Gates. You would think he is always working on computers. No, he's not. He and his wife are traipsing around the world, the Bill and Linda Gates Foundation, and they are not only in favor of birth control, but he wants to promote a birth control chip. Then they control via the chip as to whether or not you can have babies. He's also big on creating vaccines, but he is being sued by many different countries because his so-called vaccines to help people are killing more people than helping them.

But even Bill Gates, in a recent interview admitted that we really need this death panel discussion although we're not supposed to know that. It's costing the system too much money and we are going to have to make the choice whether or not we want to invest that money in paying teachers or knocking off your loved one who deserves to die.

Bill Gates: *"So we are spending at a huge rate, which if it wasn't increasing faster than inflation, it's increasing at a percentage of the economy, then you could probably afford it. But as it continues to grow, it squeezes, unless some people say they would like to be taxed a lot more, and in most states, they have these super majorities that are required to do that, it's not clearly a good thing either. But as long as you're dealing with a finite amount, as the medical cost goes up and that shows up both in state budgets is so-called state Medicaid spending, and it shows up in the federal budget as Medicare and they're part of Medicaid. It squeezes out everything else so right now what you see is it's squeezing higher education. You're raising tuitions at the University of California as rapidly as they can, so that the excess that used to be available to the middle class or whatever, it's just rapidly going away.*

"That is the trade-off society's making because of very, very, high medical costs. And the lack of willingness to say, is spending a million dollars on that last three months of life for that patient, would it be better not to lay off those 10 teachers and to make that trade up in medical costs but that's called the death panel and you're not supposed to have that discussion."

That's pretty sick. Now of all things to do when you step down from your computer magnate, that got you so rich, why would you be so interested in population control issues? Well, wait until you see who his dad worked for.

Bill Gates: *"One issue that really grabbed me as urgent, is population, reproductive health."*

Bill Moyers: *"Did you come to reproductive issues as an intellectual?"*

Bill Gates: *"As I was growing up my parents were always involved in various volunteer things. Dad was the head of Planned Parenthood. And it was very controversial to be involved in that."*

So that is why you became a billionaire and you use that influence to continue that death mentality. His dad was the head of Planned Parenthood. Full circle folks, it starts with abortion, you roll over and you let them kill babies inside the womb, that leads to euthanasia, and death panels, and that's happening right now. You can kill adults outside the womb and again this was warned 15-20 years ago. And God warned 2,000 years ago. This is the murder, anemeros, wholesale murder in our society when you turn away from God in the last days.

I don't want to get into genetic manipulation, but the other thing that Dr. Nathanson warned about, remember the term, they want to live forever, to achieve immortality. But he talked about test tube babies. I just want to forecast for you, if you think this is going to be wild, what is coming next is what you call designer babies. Have you seen in the media, it's already started, it's soft disclosure, they are getting us used to it? Now you can decide if your baby has blue eyes, is it a boy or a girl, now it is moving towards, do you want super intelligence, each one of these is like an accessory on your car. More money!

They are also talking about the longevity of life. Not only your genes but what happens if your heart runs out? What are you going to do? Well, this leads to the mindset of the test tube babies, i.e. the issue of cloning. I'm telling you what is coming next. You might call me crazy, but I warn you, what is coming next is that when they clone people they will try to convince us that these people are not people so that we can harvest their body parts, like a crop, and that is what the rich people can buy to keep themselves from dying. Actual human body parts. You might think that the cloning thing went away with Dolly the sheep. No, it has never gone away and it's not going away. You thought it was only the sheep, listen to this. They have already cloned, camel, carp, sheep, cat, cattle, coyote, dog, fruit flies, bison, goats, horses, mice, monkeys, rams, mules, pigs, rabbits, gazelles, and an artic wolf. They are cloning all kinds of things. And, that would include people.

They have two different terms of human cloning. One is Therapeutic Cloning; the other is Reproductive Cloning. These are medical terms already out there. Therapeutic Cloning would involve cells from a human for use in medicine and transplants. Reproductive Cloning would involve making an entire cloned human, instead of just the specific cells and tissues, because now you can get their body parts. They are going to try to convince us that that is not a real person, just like they say that's not a real baby, it's just a blob of tissue. In order to make a human you still need a sperm and an egg, even if it is in a test tube. But God is the author of life. That is a real human, but they will convince us, no it's not a real baby, it's a blob of tissue, no, that's not a human, that's a clone. It doesn't even have a soul. Let's harvest them like a crop. I'm telling you, that is what is coming next. This has already been going on for many, many decades.

In 2004 and 2005 in South Korea, at the Seoul University, they made a breakthrough in human cloning. In 2018, just last year, they had their two successful clonings of primates, two live females, perfect clones. Advocates support the development of therapeutic cloning in order to generate tissues and whole organs to treat patients who otherwise could not obtain transplants. Why? Remember we were warned about this, 15-20 years ago in of all places *Focus on the Family*. "*To stave off the effects of aging. Reproductive cloning could be prone to abuse and leading to a generation of humans whose organs and tissues could be harvested. Religious groups are divided.*" What's the division here? That's a human. All murder is wrong. Be it a baby inside the womb, a baby outside the womb, a young child outside the womb, a teenager outside the womb, an adult outside the womb, or a human that God made in a test tube. Now you are thinking, 'Come on, we would never get to the point where we would literally harvest people's organs while they are alive, would we?' It has been going on for many years in China. Here is what one doctor had to say.

"I am a doctor and I spent thirty years helping and saving patients. I never thought that I would spend ten years of my life investigating how doctors killed innocent human beings."

"Shun Jun Hospital of the Second Military University in Shanghai reported that within three years, from 2003 to 2006 this hospital did 120 cases of emergency liver transplants. The fastest of which was within 4 hours of admission. It was cited as a miracle in medical history. There is surely a possibility that they had a supply of people whom could be killed for their organs anytime it's needed. Only

under such a condition could they make this emergency liver transplant happen within hours."

TV Chosun reports: "*No wonder trafficking was suspected. And then a doctor in China escaped and exposed the horrors of organ extraction."*

Dr Enver Tohti: "*At the Western Mountain Execution Ground, I was surprised, when I cut through, blood still came out. That is to say, blood is still running. That means this person is still alive. And the gun shot wound is to the right, not to the left. So that is to say to make sure this person is not dead. I cut through to the both sides, removed the liver and two kidneys. It took me less than 30 minutes. They shot them in the right chest so as not to damage organs. And I extracted their organs while they were still alive."*

Information from other witnesses:

"I was in Beijing when the crackdown occurred. I watched it happen. I didn't know what I was seeing. It was very disturbing."

"It's a huge population, extremely vulnerable. This becomes a sea of expendable humanity."

"The year of 2005. A patient of mine came to me one afternoon and told me that 'Doctor, I am scheduled to get a heart transplantation.' And I looked at him and said, 'How can they schedule a heart transplantation two weeks ahead of time?"

"I was in Beijing for three years. Every three hours we got a lab test."

"No one in the mainstream media inside China are saying, they are covering up what is going on. It is one of the most catastrophic human rights violations in our time. After I left China, my perspective totally changed. I thought, Oh, my God, I committed a crime."

"According to two Chinese News outlets in the U.S., the Epic Times and NTD TV, two witnesses had testified there was a concentration camp in SuJiaTun China. Thousands of Falun Gong practitioners were imprisoned there, and their organs were harvested by doctors."

"My ex-husband and I worked in this hospital from 1999 to 2004. I want to apologize on behalf of my ex-husband because he was a neurological surgeon who harvested organs from these Falun Gong practitioners. I heard from my ex-husband that most of them had strong bodies. When their organs were harvested, they still had breath. After their organs were harvested, their bodies were thrown into the incinerator without any trace left."

Isn't that what Hitler did with the Jews? Do you see why God's wrath is going to come? Did you see how they actually had medical tests? How's your kidneys by the way? How's your eyesight? Why? In case you're are a match for some rich person. Aren't you glad the government is taking over our healthcare? And one of the mandates of that healthcare is to make all of our medical records electronic and searchable in a giant database. And aren't you glad we are all hooked on providing, voluntarily, our DNA samples? It's just to find out your ancestry. That's all they will use that DNA sample for. Sounds weird, but we have come full circle. You start off by killing kids alive in the womb, and you harvested their body parts for medical purposes, even for anti-aging purposes. Now you're killing adults alive outside the womb to harvest their body parts for medical purposes. It's not coming here is it?

CNN reports: *"It's the second time Jacqueline Johnson cried next to her son, Kendrick's grave. The first time he was being lowered into the ground. This time he is being pulled out of it."*

Reporter: *"Did you ever think you would have to exhume his body?*

Ms. Johnson: *"No, not after they buried his body."*

Reporter: *"In June, Kendrick's body was sent to Florida. The Johnson's hired Dr. Bill Anderson to conduct a second independent autopsy. In that autopsy, Dr. Anderson told the Johnson's that Kendrick died as a result of a blow to the neck and not accidental asphyxia after slipping into a rolled gym mat at school as investigators in Georgia had said. But what Dr. Anderson did not find shocked them."*

Dr. Anderson: *"When we got the body for the second autopsy, the heart, lungs, liver were not with the body, the brain, they were all absent."*

Reporter: "*Every organ, from the top of Kendrick's head to his pelvis, gone. And his family had no idea.*"

In the United States of America! They lied about his death and said he was asphyxiated, got stuck in a mat. No, he was murdered by somebody hitting him in the back of the neck. Now his body parts are gone. In the United States of America. We need to speak up on this issue of abortion. Because you are already beginning to see the future of us, for decades now, of keeping our mouths shut. It's not only the cause of the 1.5 billion children and growing, but when you speak up on this issue, it might be your own life that you are working at saving. Because if they deem that you are mentally deficient or if you just happen to be a good match for somebody, don't think that they won't come and get you. It sounds sick, but this is what is going on. And we shouldn't be surprised because Jesus warned us 2,000 years ago, in the last days, a brutal, sickening, anemeros, murderous wholesale slaughter society is going to appear on the scene. And you wonder why His wrath will be poured out for 7 years non-stop? This is the future and we need to speak up on this today.

How to Receive Jesus Christ:

1. Admit your need (I am a sinner).

2. Be willing to turn from your sins (repent).

3. Believe that Jesus Christ died for you on the Cross and rose from the grave.

4. Through prayer, invite Jesus Christ to come in and control your life through the Holy Spirit. (Receive Him as Lord and Savior.)

What to pray:

Dear Lord Jesus,

I know that I am a sinner and need Your forgiveness. I believe that You died for my sins. I want to turn from my sins. I now invite You to come into my heart and life. I want to trust and follow You as Lord and Savior.

In Jesus' name. Amen.

Notes

Chapter 1 *The History of Abortion*

1. *The Voice of John*
   https://wwwvoiceofjohn.org
2. *Senators who voted against Bill protecting born-alive babies*
   https://aclj.org/pro-life/naming-names-44-senators-who-voted-in-favor-of-infanticide-and-protecting-born-alive-babies
3. *Evolution leads to Hitler & abortion*
   https://www.youtube.com/watch?v=MNC8jVceJ9o

Chapter 2 *The Motive of Abortion*

1. *The Voice of John*
   https://wwwvoiceofjohn.org
2. *Harvesting Fetal Body Parts*
   https://www.dailysignal.com//print?post_id=261025
   https://www.nrlc.org/archive/Baby_Parts/omeara.html
3. *Fetal tissue: How it's used in medical research*
   https://www/cnn.com/2015/07/17health/fetal-tissue-explainer/index.html
4. *Who buys, sells and uses fetal tissue acquired from abortion clinics*
   https://www.seatletimes.com/nation-world/who-buys-sells-and-uses-fetal-tissue-acquired-from-abortion-clinics/
5. *Baby Parts used for Vaccines*
   https://www.youtube.com/watch?v=PN7FQCkiBp8
6. *Chelsea Clinton says stopping abortion is unchristian*
   https://www.youtube.com/watch?v=WdHC7yoIkZY
7. *Cuomo signs abortion rights bill*
   https://www.youtube.com/watch?v=hiMuZv9k_x0
8. *Trump addresses paid family leave, abortion at State of the Union*

https://www.youtube.com/watch?v=FlIPjK5rVWs
9. *Trump pushes anti-abortion agenda*
https://www.youtube.com/watch?v=awrtQg27oZ0

Chapter 3 *The Church & Abortion*

1. *The Voice of John*
https://wwwvoiceofjohn.org
2. *Religious Leaders Bless Opening of New Planned Parenthood Abortion Clinic*
https://www.lifenews.com/2017/01/12/religious-leaders-bless-opening-of-new- planned-parenthood-abortion-clinic-call-it-sacred-work/
3. *Word of Faith Televangelist urged vasectomies*
http://www.presstelegram.com/general-news/20141025/reports-televangelist-urged-vasectomies-abortion
4. *Presbyterian Minister Blesses Planned Parenthood Clinic*
http://pulpitandpen.org/2018/05/16/Presbyterian-minister-blesses-planned-parenthood-clinic-serves-as-clinic-chaplain/
5. *Americans Confused about abortion*
www.georgebarna.com/research-flow/2017/9/27/americans-confused-about-abortion
6. *Ex-abortion Doctor tells the shocking truth about abortion*
https://www.youtube.com/watch?v=A16gzm9eaa8
7. *Hillsong pastor, Carl Lentz compromises on murdering children*
https://www.youtube.com/watch?v=JIaUmGiuGQ4
8. *Speak out "Blessing" at abortion clinic*
https://www.youtube.com/watch?v=gTYL0LtaghE
9. *Speak out abortion clinic*
https://www.youtube.com/watch?v=yf2tA84Q8sQ

Chapter 4 *The Survivors of Abortion*

1. *Moloch*
https://en.wikipedia.org/wiki/Moloch
2. *East Village Doctor Convicted of Performing Illegal Abortion*
https://www.nytimes.com/1993/02/23/nyregion/east-village-doctor-convicted-

of-performing-illegal-abortion-html
3. *Gianna Jessen* https://en.wikipedia.org/wiki/Gianna_Jessen
4. *Melissa Ohden* https://en.wikipedia.org/wiki/Melissa_Ohden
5. *Chairman Goodlatte question to Pricilla Smith* https://www.youtube.com/watch?v=oIXDx0pJF38
6. *Gianna Jessen's powerful abortion survival story* https://www.youtube.com/watch?v=pwpJTY1pEns
7. *Melissa Ohden an abortion survivor* https://www.youtube.com/watch?v=3adLns91_SQ
8. *Ana Rosa Rodriguez* https://www.youtube.com/watch?v=_ihijgw5pe8
9. *Virginia Democrat defends bill* https://www.youtube.com/watch?v=K9KkAqPv_AI
10. *Virginia governor Ralph Northam on killing live born babies* https://www.youtube.com/watch?v=_xD8cPgcZ3E
11. *What is 4D ultrasound* https://www.youtube.com/watch?v=OBV7i9zRAto

Chapter 5 *The Aftermath of Abortion*

1. *By the numbers: U.S. Abortion Statistics* https://www.focusonthefamily.com/socialissues/life-issues/dignity-of-human-life/abortion-statistics
2. *Facts about abortion* https://abort73.com/abortion_facts/us_abortion_statistics/
3. *The moral dilemma of repeat abortions* https://abort73.com/blog/the_moral_dilemma_of_repeat_abortion/
4. *Abortion Statistics* https://www.all.org/learn/abortion/abortion-statistics/
5. *Induced Abortion Worldwide* https://www.guttmacher.org/fact-sheet/induced-abortion-worldwide?gclid=EAlalQobChMix4ql9sed4QIVFQOGCh3CsQUCEAAYASAAEglao_D_Bwe
6. *Abortion doctor growling and saying he love killing babies* https://www.youtube.com/watch?v=ds9rxB6akLM
7. *Beto supports 3rd trimester abortions*

https://www.youtube.com/watch?v=WLSmlNgkbk4

Chapter 6 *The Response to Abortion*

1. *Washington State to Churches; Pay for Abortions or Break the Law* www1.cbn.com/cbnnews/us/2019/march/Washington-state-to-churches-pay-for-abortions-or-break-the-law?fbclid=IwAR1f2NSTO7plps-tWnbj9bTtl1
2. *Abortion Terminology* https://carm.org/abortion-terminology
3. *Fetal Development Pictures* https://www.webmd.com/baby/ss/slideshow-fetal-development
4. *Abortion Procedures* https://carm.org/abortion-procedures
5. *The battle over words in the abortion discussion* https://carm.org/battle-over-words-abortion-discussion
6. *What does the Bible say about abortion?* https://carm.org/what-does-the-bible-say-about-abortion
7. *Why abortion is wrong* https://carm.org/why-abortion-is-wrong
8. *Arguments supporting abortion* https://carm.org/refuting-arguments-supporting-abortion
9. *Abortion pros and cons* https://abortion.procon.org
10. *Pro-life answers to pro-choice arguments* https://www.campaiglifecoalition.com/pro-life-answers
11. *Abortion is legal, and Christians should submit to the government* https://carm.org.abortion-legal
12. *Abortion is the leading cause of death worldwide in 2018* https://www.lifenews.com/2018/12/31/abortion-was-the-leading-cause-of-death-worldwide-in-2018-killing-42-million-people/?fbclid=iwar2rtwsxig9x
13. *Kentucky banned abortion* https://www.aclu.org/blog/reproductive-freedom/abortion/Kentucky-just-banned-abortion?fbclid=iwar3dbitpfo15j8vsr-mtf9h5i91s7vxgxe07hvv337s
14. *Georgia is latest state to pass fetal heartbeat bill* https://www.nytimes.com/2019/03/30/us/Georgia-fetal-heartbeat-abortion-law.html
15. *Actors consider boycott of Georgia* https://www.nydailynews.com/news/national/ny-news-hollywood-actors-

boycott-georgia-heartbeat-abortion-bill-20190401-ti3xraihkja7jea6zilu7aiyqm
16. *Alyssa Milano on Twitter* https://twitter.com/Alyssa_Milano/status/1111231181314510849/photo /1?ref_src=twsrc%7ctwcamp%5etweetembed%7ctwterm%5e11112311
17. *Virginia Governor signs bill to make Animal cruelty a felony* https://www.lifenews.com/2019/04/02virginia-governor-who-supported-infanticide-signs-bill-to-make-animal-cruelty-a-felony/?fbclid= iwar3xt4ziqv_ri
18. *Iceland kills almost 100% of babies with down syndrome* http://www.lifenews.com/2019/03/23/Iceland-kills-almost-100-of-babies-with-down-syndrome-in-abortion-denmark-98-france-77-andu-s-67/
19. *Taxpayer Funding of Abortion at Planned Parenthood* https://www.youtube.com/watch?v=Icz-nyjXsWw
20. *Washington State to churches 'Pay for Abortions'* https://www.youtube.com/watch?v=0jzDcTVT4P0
21. *Cedar Park Church* Y2mate.com-cedar_park_church_sb6219_will_force_washington_church

Chapter 7 *The Future of Abortion Part 1*

1. *Abortion survivor exposes Planned Parenthood* https://www.youtube.com/watch?v=0jzDcTVT4P0
2. *Backlash grows against VA governor* https://www.youtube.com/watch?v=K9KkAqPv_AI&t=69s
3. *Ben Sasse, all babies have dignity* https://www.youtube.com/watch?v=u5w1Rnq8n2A
4. *Dean Cain reacts* https://www.youtube.com/watch?v=nPVnQHi1jXA
5. *Ben Sasse, This is infanticide* https://www.youtube.com/watch?v=tMTJZMHRM6U
6. *Senate Rejects the Born-Alive Abortion Survivors* https://www.youtube.com/watch?v=4TcBmlRLIl4
7. *Nurse witnessed aborted babies born alive* https://www.youtube.com/watch?v=7RfKoex_4vI
8. *Stacy Abrams, Bill is bad for business* https://www.youtube.com/watch?v=qK_b2zuQ2J0

Chapter 8 *The Future of Abortion Part 2*

1. *The word euthanasia*
   https://all.org/learn/euthanasia/definitions/
2. *Assisted suicides in the United States*
   https://en.wikipedia.org/wiki/assisted_suicide_in_the_united_states
3. *New push for physician assisted suicide bill in NY*
   https://wbng.com/news/2019/01/26/new-push-for-physician-assisted-suicide-bill-in-ny-2/?fbclid=iwar0gkumxoui18ysgmzzfc_osdfcl_fyogbejpugh
4. *Assisted suicide spreading across the world*
   https://en.wikipedia.org/wiki/assisted_suicide
5. *Terminally ill children, ages 9 and 11, euthanized in Belgium*
   https://nypost.com/2018/08/08/terminally-ill-children-ages-9-11-euthanized-in-Belgium/
6. *Euthanasia & assisted suicide: Canada gets ready to apply it to children*
   https://www.nationalreview.com/2018/11/Canada-euthanasia-assisted-suicide-children
7. *Toronto hospital releases assisted suicide plan for kids*
   https://www1.cbn.com/cbnnews/world/2018/October/Toronto-hospital-realeses-assisted-suicide-plan-for-kids-may-not-even-inform-parents
8 *Obamacare death panels should be ended*
   https://www.washingtontimes.com/news/2017/jun/14/Obamacare-death-panels-should-be-ended/
9. *List of animals that have been cloned*
   https://en.wikipedia.org/wiki/list_of_animals_that_have_been_cloned
10. *Human Cloning*
   https://en.wikipedia.org/wiki/human_cloning